Daniel and the NATO Connection

Daniel and the NATO Connection

A Biblical Exposition of Daniel and
the Transformation of NATO

by

Allen Bonck

iUniverse, Inc.
Bloomington

Daniel and the NATO Connection
A Biblical Exposition of Daniel and the Transformation of NATO

iUniverse books may be ordered through booksellers or by contacting:

iUniverse
1663 Liberty Drive
Bloomington, IN 47403
www.iuniverse.com
1-800-Authors (1-800-288-4677)

Because of the dynamic nature of the Internet, any web addresses or links contained in this book may have changed since publication and may no longer be valid. The views expressed in this work are solely those of the author and do not necessarily reflect the views of the publisher, and the publisher hereby disclaims any responsibility for them.

Bible references are from the King James Bible.
Book graphics are by author.

ISBN: 978-1-4697-8591-2 (sc)
ISBN: 978-1-4697-8592-9 (hc)
ISBN: 978-1-4697-8593-6 (e)

Printed in the United States of America

iUniverse rev. date: 02/29/2012

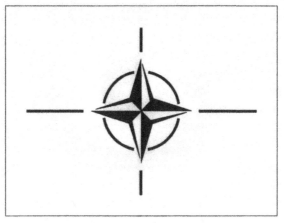

NATO flag

DEDICATION

To Pastor Robert Hooley, who was my instructor when I was a young Bible college student and provided me with a foundation of scriptural understanding and inspiration to study biblical prophecy for all these years.

SYMBOL GLOSSARY

A glossary of the symbols used at the start of each chapter.

Chapter One: The symbol represents the great image of King Nebuchadnezzar's dream. The head represents Nebuchadnezzar's Babylonian Empire, which existed from 612 BC through 539 BC.

Chapter Two: The symbol is a he-goat with a large, notable horn between its eyes. The goat represents Alexander the Great and his kingdom. The great horn will break, and four lesser horns will replace it.

Chapter Three: The symbol is meant to represent the North Atlantic Treaty Organization (NATO), which represents the ten commanders of the final military alliance of this world, which will rise from the old Roman Empire.

Chapter Four: The symbol is the Assyrian star, as seen in the center of the new Assyrian flag. The star represents the ethnic Assyrian Persian king, which comes from modern-day Iran.

Chapter Five: The symbol represents the ten horns and ten pseudo-kings of the beast's kingdom. The 666 is the number of the beast's name, used to identify his followers.

Chapter Six: The symbol is a woman and represents Babylon the Great. She sits upon the beast and his empire.

Chapter Seven: The symbol represents the new Jewish temple, which will be built on the temple mount in Jerusalem.

CONTENTS

A DESCRIPTIVE OUTLINE

Chapter One: "Daniel 2" (pages 3-19) studies a dream that Nebuchadnezzar, king of Babylon, had in the second year of his reign. The dream reveals the sequence of world empires, starting with Nebuchadnezzar's Babylonian Empire and continuing until the God of heaven establishes his kingdom on earth. These empires are studied both by Scripture and through world history. This sequence, through Daniel and his God-given interpretation, is so accurate that many scholars believe that it could have been written only after the events happened. The study looks into the gap in time between the Roman Empire and the coming end-time manifestation of the final empires, which are shown in the dream as two feet and ten toes. The chapter includes a time chart and maps of the world empires.

Chapter Two: "Daniel 8" (pages 21-31) studies Daniel's vision of the daily sacrifice and transgression of desolation. The vision clarifies the identity of several of the sequential empires of Daniel 2. The vision introduces us to the "little horn," a king of fierce countenance who will rule the world at the end of the age. He fights the Prince of princes and is defeated by the Lord of hosts. This vision also establishes the great end-time sign of the abomination of desolation, which is referenced by Jesus in the New Testament Gospels. The little horn is also linked to the last days' restored Jewish temple on the temple mount in Jerusalem.

Chapter Three: "Daniel 7" (pages 33-50) studies the dreams and visions that Daniel received in the first year of Belshazzar, king of Babylon. A sequence of great beasts rise up out of the great sea (Mediterranean Sea), each represented and characterized by an animal. These beasts represent empires that exist contemporary to each other in the last days. They are shown to fall into the time frame of the two feet and ten toes of Daniel 2.

A contemporary fulfillment is offered and explained. The empires are shown to be England (Great Britain), the lion; the Soviet Union (Russia), the bear; the nation of Islam, a restored Islamic caliphate coming from the Middle East, the leopard; and a military alliance rising from the old Roman Empire, having a command structure of ten generals. The military alliance is believed to be the transformation of NATO, the North Atlantic Treaty Organization.

Chapter Four: "Daniel 11" (pages 51-63) studies a vision that Daniel receives from an angel of God. The vision shows what will befall Daniel's people (Jewish people) in the last days. The vision indicates there will be a series of four kings rising from Persia (modern-day Iran). Ultimately, the fourth and final king is identified as the king who sets up the abomination of desolation in the Jewish temple at Jerusalem. He is the little horn, the king who fights the Prince of princes and is defeated by the Lord of hosts. The Messiah goes to Edom (southern Jordan) to deliver a remnant of Jews from that area. The Messiah then travels to Jerusalem to confront and defeat the fourth Persian king. The fourth king is shown to be Persian by citizenship and Assyrian by ethnicity.

Chapter Five: "Revelation 17" (pages 65-87) studies the following chapters of the book of Revelation: 12, 13, 17, 18, and 19. The primary focus is on understanding the beast with seven heads and ten horns and its relationship to the great whore, Babylon the Great. This chapter will identify who the woman is and coordinate the prophecies of Revelation with Daniel and his visions. Several charts are included in this chapter.

Chapter Six: "Babylon the Great" (pages 89-99) studies the subject of end-time Babylon, as found not only in Revelation but also the books of Isaiah, Jeremiah, and Ezekiel. There are many faces of Babylon— economic, religious, spiritual, and national—but this study looks only at national Babylon. There is only one nation that fits all the scriptural descriptions: America. America and NATO fit together exactly as shown in Scripture. Rome also is considered in this chapter.

Chapter Seven: "Things to Come" (pages 101-112) looks at events and circumstances that will come to pass in the near future:

- The Jewish temple, to be located on the temple mount in Jerusalem
- NATO transformation—the amazing transformation and actions of NATO
- American and European relations; American/European relations will deteriorate into open conflict
- The coming Iranian/Assyrian leader—the amazing restoration of an Assyrian nation in Iraq and the leader who rises up from there
- The Islamic caliphate—the attempt by Iran and other Muslim nations to create a worldwide Islamic caliphate
- The wife—the bride of Christ and her preparation to go to heaven and return with Christ as his wife and part of his army

Indexes and Summaries: Informational summaries are included within the chapters to aid the reader in studying and referencing information and Scriptures. The following indexes are provided at back of the book:

- General Index
- Index of Names
- Index of Places
- Scripture Index

INTRODUCTION

This book is designed to harmonize the biblical books of Daniel and Revelation, to paint a picture of the events of the end-times—the times in which we now live. Prophetic events have unfolded—and currently are unfolding—right before our eyes. The organization currently known as NATO, the North Atlantic Treaty Organization, could play a pivotal role, through a series of transformations, in fulfilling the world's prophetic future, as found in Scripture. To fully appreciate these events, we need to know what to look for. I believe that we are living in an unprecedented time, a time that men of the past have desired to see, and the time of the soon manifestation of the kingdom of God. Every devoted Christian has prayed the words, "thy kingdom come, thy will be done in earth as it is in heaven."

If, indeed, we mean what we pray, then we truly must be excited and amazed at the faithfulness of God as we see his kingdom coming. To see God's kingdom come also means that the kingdoms and systems of this world must be dealt with, and the judgment of sin and removal of the ungodly must be a part of God's process. This is referenced in Acts 17:11.

> Because he [God] hath appointed a day in which he will judge the world in righteousness by that man whom he hath ordained; whereof he hath given assurance unto all men, in that he hath raised him from the dead.

Most of Daniel's visions and dreams end with the establishment of God's kingdom, which will have no end.

The book of Daniel is the kingpin of understanding the prophetic events of the last days. Virtually all of the major events are seen in Daniel's visions, to some extent. Today, we refer to terms such as "the seventieth week," or the "little horn," or even the "abomination of desolation," all of which have their origins in Daniel's visions or dreams.

For the student of biblical prophecy, an understanding the book of Daniel is a must. If you can come to grips with Daniel, you can build a much clearer picture of how events relate to each other and harmonize them with the writings of other prophets and biblical books.

CHAPTER ONE

Daniel 2

In the second year of the reign of Nebuchadnezzar, the king dreamed a dream. It was the start of an incredible series of events for both the king and the young man Daniel. Daniel and other young men of the children of Israel were brought as captives from Judea to Babylon. They were to be taught the knowledge and tongue of the Chaldeans.

Nebuchadnezzar's dream woke him up, and it bothered him. He called for the magicians, astrologers, sorcerers, and the Chaldeans to interpret the dream for him. He had forgotten the dream, however, because he said, "The thing is gone from me." So he not only required an interpretation but also the dream itself. This request would not be a problem if the Chaldeans could contact the source of the dream.

A dream can come from several different sources—the dreamer's own heart, mind, or spirit; or an external source, such as a spirit or an angel. The king had called for the men in his kingdom whom he felt could contact the source of the dream and ascertain an answer to his questions. It needs to be noted that magicians, astrologers, sorcerers, and Chaldeans all used divinations to enter into and converse with the spirit realm. The use of divinations is a practice strictly forbidden by the God of the Bible (Deut. 18:9–12), and he would never respond to their requests. If the source of the dream had come from a spiritual source that they could contact, and they had the ransom that would be required by that source for the information (a price must be paid; nothing is free, not even in the spiritual realm), they would be able to help the king. If the Chaldeans could get the king to tell them the dream, they could conjure (make up) an interpretation. But the king would not or could not tell them the dream. In the end, the Chaldeans, astrologers, magicians, and sorcerers had no help for the king, and the king, in his anger, condemned all of them to death. **They obviously had no contact with the source of the dream**. The king included Daniel and the other children of Israel with the Chaldeans, so unless Daniel and his friends could get an answer for the king, they also would be executed.

It's important for us to know that this dream and its interpretation were indeed from the God of heaven and not some inferior source. Daniel sought God through prayer and received the dream and interpretation, and this is what he had to say:

> I thank thee, and praise thee, O thou God of my fathers, who hast given me wisdom and might, and hast made known unto me now what we desired of thee: for thou hast now made known unto us the king's matter. (2:23)

When Daniel came before the king he was confident that he knew all, and indeed he did. The king acknowledged the dream and exalted Daniel and his friends, Shadrach, Meshach, and Abednego, into high positions within his government.

As it turns out, this dream reaches far beyond Nebuchadnezzar and the times of his kingdom, even reaching a time when God himself will set up a kingdom that shall never end.

The following is the text of the dream:

> 2:31 Thou , O king, sawest, and behold a great image. This great image, whose brightness was excellent, stood before thee; and the form thereof was terrible. (32)This image's head was of fine gold, his breast and his arms of silver, his belly and his thighs of brass, (33) his legs of iron, his feet part of iron and part of clay. (34) Thou sawest till that a stone was cut out without hands, which smote the image upon his feet that were of iron and clay, and brake them to pieces. (35)

Then was the iron, and the clay, the brass, the silver, and the gold, broken to pieces together, and become like chaff of the summer threshing floors; and the wind carried them away, that no place was found for them: and the stone that smote the image became a great mountain, and filled the whole earth. (36) This is the dream; and we will tell the interpretation thereof before the king.

The dream appears to be a very straightforward vision of a large figure, like a man, standing in front of Nebuchadnezzar. Scripture says that it was terrible and uses the Aramaic word *"deh-khal,* which means something to be feared, with the connotation of terror. This would explain why the king was so troubled by the vision. Another aspect that would have troubled the king was the violence of the destruction of the image. It was smote by a stone. Again, the Scripture uses an Aramaic word, *mekh-aw,* which means to strike, smite, and kill. The image comes crashing down and is blown away by a mighty wind. This wind would have been completely supernatural and the chaff of the image completely blown away until "no place was found for them."

The image may have looked like man in terms of its parts—head, arms, legs, etc.—but that is where the similarity ends. No man has a head made of gold, or a breast and arms of silver, or a belly and thighs of brass. This image was not meant to be a man but to <u>represent</u> something more. The feet and toes of clay and iron were the weak points of the image and the location of its demise. It is obvious that the stone that was cut out <u>without hands</u> is a very special and powerful part of the vision. After the image is destroyed completely, the stone becomes a "great mountain" and fills the <u>whole</u> earth.

I would like to make note here of the personal character of the man Daniel. He makes sure that the king understands that Daniel represents the children of Israel and that he is not acting as an individual. Daniel obviously wants to save not only himself from execution but also his fellow children of Israel. He does this by referring to "we" in verse 36: "and we will tell the interpretation thereof before the king."

The description of the dream, as seen in verses 31–36, represents only the first part of the king's requirement. Daniel continues with an interpretation:

(37) Thou, O king, art a king of kings: for the God of heaven hath given thee a kingdom, power, and strength, and glory. (38) And wheresoever the children of men dwell, the beasts of the field and the fowls of the heaven hath he given into thine hand, and hath made thee ruler over them all. Thou art this head of gold. (39) And after thee shall arise another kingdom inferior to thee, and another third kingdom of brass, which shall bear rule over all the earth. (40) And the fourth kingdom shall be strong as iron: forasmuch as iron breaketh in pieces and subdueth all things: and as iron that breaketh all these, shall it break in pieces and bruise.(41) And whereas thou sawest the feet and toes, part of potters' clay, and part of iron, the kingdom shall be divided; but there shall be in it of the strength of iron, forasmuch as thou sawest the iron mixed with miry clay. (42) And as the toes of the feet were part of iron, and part of clay, so the kingdom shall be partly strong, and partly broken. (43) And whereas thou sawest iron mixed with miry clay, they shall mingle themselves with the seed of men: but they shall not cleave one to another, even as iron is not mixed with clay. (44) And in the days of these kings shall the God of heaven set up a kingdom, which shall never be destroyed: and the kingdom shall not be left to other people, but it shall break in pieces and consume all these kingdoms, and it shall stand for ever. (45) Forasmuch as thou sawest that the stone was cut out of the mountain without hands, and that it brake in pieces the iron, the brass, the clay, the silver, and the gold; the great God hath made known to the king what shall come to pass hereafter: and the dream is certain, and the interpretation thereof sure.

The first point made in this interpretation is that the head of gold represents a kingdom—not just any kingdom but Nebuchadnezzar's kingdom. (See map of Babylon Empire on page 14.) Daniel 2:1 states that the dream came to Nebuchadnezzar in the second year of his reign. This indicated that he would be great not because of what he had done but rather because of what he would do. The vision was looking at what the Babylonian kingdom would become under Nebuchadnezzar's rule—he would be a king of kings.

It's clear from this dream that God thought highly of Nebuchadnezzar and the kingdom he would govern. In addition, the king clearly was a pagan and worshipped many gods and even required his subjects to bow down to an image that he himself made. Later, in Daniel 4, God chastised him because of his pride and arrogance.

> 4:30 The king spake, and said, is not this great Babylon, that I have built for the house of the kingdom by the might of my power, and for the honour of my majesty? (31) While the word was in the king's mouth, there fell a voice from heaven, saying, O king Nebuchadnezzar, to thee it is spoken; the kingdom is departed from thee.

The king was driven from dwelling with men into the wilderness with the beasts of the field. With the passing of time, he looked up to heaven and blessed the most high, and God returned his sanity and reason to him and he was restored to his kingdom.

> At the same time my reason returned unto me; and for the glory of my kingdom, mine honour and brightness returned unto me; and my counselors and my lords sought unto me; and I was established in my kingdom, and excellent majesty was added unto me. (37) Now I, Nebuchadnezzar, praise and extol and honour the King of heaven, all whose works are truth, and his ways judgment: and those that walk in pride he is able to abase. (Dan. 4:36–37)

King Nebuchadnezzar not only was a great leader and administrator, but he also was teachable. I have included this story of Nebuchadnezzar because it is **important to understand that God knows and uses the kings and leaders of this world to accomplish his desires and will in this earth.** We should never limit the effect of God on and in the affairs of our leaders.

Nebuchadnezzar's kingdom comes to an end under the control of his son Belshazzar; his story is seen in Daniel 5. Belshazzar has a great feast, and during the party and the drinking, he commands that the temple vessels (which had been dedicated to God's worship and service) be brought out and used to drink and worship other gods—the gods of gold, silver, brass, iron, wood, and stone. While they were drinking, a finger of a man's hand manifested and wrote a message on the wall in the palace, under the light of a candlestick. No one at the party could read the message. Belshazzar called for the Chaldeans, astrologers, and soothsayers to give him the interpretation of the writing. They could not help the king, because they had no contact with the source of the message. They eventually brought Daniel to interpret the message, which he did. The message was *mene, mene, tekel, upharsin.*

> This is the interpretation of the thing: MENE; God hath numbered thy kingdom, and finished it. (27) TEKEL; Thou art weighed in the balances, and art found wanting. (28) PERES; Thy kingdom is divided, and given to the Medes and Persians...... (30) In that night was Belshazzar, the king of the Chaldeans, slain. (31) And Darius the Median took the Kingdom. (5:26–31)

Again, the source of the message is from the God of heaven, and in the writing of this message, he has identified the next kingdom to replace Babylon. **That kingdom is the Medes and Persians, the breast and two arms of silver.** (See maps of Median and Persian Empires on pages 15 & 16.)

While the Medes and Persians became a very large and powerful kingdom—certainly much larger than the Babylonians—God indicated (Dan. 2:39) that they were inferior to the Babylonian Empire. It's clear that the size or power of a kingdom is not how God measures kingdoms.

The Persian Empire continued until approximately 331 BC During the earlier stages of the Persian Empire, they invaded Macedonia and Greece. They were not completely successful in their control—when they were forced to retreat into Cappadocia (modern-day Turkey), they were brutal to the Greeks and Macedonians. When the young Macedonian king Alexander the Great came to power, much of his motivation toward the Persians was retribution for this brutality. Alexander started his conquest of Persia against King Darius III and finished it with King Artexerxes. Although Alexander died at a young age, four generals took over his kingdom and continued Greek control until 63 BC, when the last Greek city fell to the Romans. **The Greek Empire, which started with Alexander the Great and ended with his four generals, is the belly and thighs of brass of Nebuchadnezzar's great image**. (See the maps of the Greek Empire on page 17.)

The Roman Empire is one of the most well known of the ancient empires. Many books and documentaries have been made about the Roman Empire and its subsequent fall. Many scholars and experts believe that the root cause of the fall was moral or spiritual corruption. Whatever the cause, the slow painful demise of the empire basically ended in AD 1458. with the fall of the eastern Roman capital of Constantinople to the Islamic caliphate known as the Ottoman Empire. The Roman Empire is known for brutal military strength and longevity—approximately fifteen hundred years. **The Roman Empire fulfills the iron kingdom of the two legs of Nebuchadnezzar's dream and represents the fifth kingdom of the image.** (See the map of Roman Empire on page 18.)

The Ottoman Empire began in the mid-1300s in the Middle East and grew to encompass most of the eastern Roman Empire. The Ottoman Empire is unique among empires in that it is the only Islamic caliphate to become so large. (See map of Ottoman Empire on page 19.) Islam does not recognize national borders; it Islam is to become a world empire and to rule all peoples, therefore sees national borders as frontiers. Islam is to conquer the land beyond these frontiers for Allah. Islam also sees any land ever held or controlled by Moslems as a part of the world Islamic caliphate, and this must be recaptured and controlled as soon as possible. Western-styled borders and governments are used today only out of convenience and would be put aside if Islam became completely dominant. The Ottomans ruled by sharia law, which is Islamic in origin. In sharia law, non-Moslems must submit to Islamic rule and become subservient to Islam. They are considered second-class citizens—they live at a slave level within Islam—and must pay special taxes to be non Moslem.. All other religious groups fall into the class of infidels.

The biblical prophets—Isaiah, Ezekiel, Jeremiah, and others—give clear indication that the Jewish people will, at some point, be restored to the land that God gave them as an inheritance. They were driven into the Diaspora (dispersion from their ancestral homeland) in AD 70

9

during the Roman Empire. During the time of the Ottoman Empire, there could be no progress toward the restoration of the Jewish people to their homeland, because Islamic law would not allow it. Until the Ottomans could be removed from their control of the Holy Land, prophecies concerning Israel and Jerusalem would be on hold—the manifestation of the two feet and the ten toes would have to wait.

The Ottoman Empire, as large as it was, did not represent the continuation of the two legs, the Eastern and Western Roman Empires. The Ottomans would lose the empire in 1919 to the western European alliance during World War I. After existing nearly five hundred years, the Ottoman Empire would be divided and sorted by the Europeans. Subsequently, many of the Middle Eastern nations, such as Egypt and Syria, would receive their independence, something that could not have happened under Ottoman sharia control.

At this point in our look at Daniel 7, we have seen only historic kingdoms and kings—things that we can find in history books—and until the arrival of the Ottoman Empire, the vision of the image was easily followed and understood. It is generally believed that the two feet and ten toes, the ones made of clay and iron, have never manifested. Let us consider what this development means. First, it is possible that the vision, no matter how accurate it had been up to the end of the Roman Empire, may not be completely true in its entirety. Or perhaps something unforeseen happened to change the final sequence. The developments that will happen during and after the two feet and ten toes are significant and will not be missed by the world at large. The ten toes are kings of a world power, and their destruction will cause the rise of God's empire/kingdom, which will grow and fill the entire world. These events certainly have not happened at this point in time.

In subsequent chapters of this book, we will study the final times of Daniel's prophecies, which will come just prior to the establishment of God's kingdom on earth. It is called the "day of the Lord" and is seen in both the Old and New Testaments. The descriptions of the events of that day echo much of what Daniel's vision reveals. The day of the Lord has not manifested as yet. So we know that if Daniel was correct when he told King Nebuchadnezzar that the dream and the interpretation was true, then we will yet see the fulfillment of the two feet and ten toes.

The good news is that Daniel had more than one vision concerning the time of the end. We will study Daniel 7 in chapter three and bridge the gap between the Roman Empire and the end.

Summary of Daniel 2

1. The God of heaven uses dreams and visions to communicate with his people (verse 19).

2. The God of heaven answers the prayers of his people. Daniel was a righteous man, and God gave him the king's dream and interpretation, thus delivering him and the children of Israel (verse 23).

3. God knows and uses kings and leaders of this world to accomplish his desires and will on this earth. Nebuchadnezzar's dream gives understanding and insight into world events for many generations. God also dealt with Nebuchadnezzar's personal character by chastising his pride (Daniel 4:30, 36 & 37).

4. The great image of Nebuchadnezzar's dream applies to a series of great empires, starting with Nebuchadnezzar's Babylon and continuing until the God of heaven sets up his kingdom, which fills the whole earth and lasts forever (verses 37–45).

5. The sequence of empires are historic, from Babylon through to the end of the Roman Empire, which ended in AD 1453, at which time the two feet and ten toes did not manifest. Instead, the Ottoman Empire (an Islamic caliphate) disrupted the sequence. The end of the Ottoman Empire in 1919 allows the progression to proceed.

6. See the Daniel 2 diagram on page xx. The diagram displays the dream and interpretation.

7. The world is still awaiting the final manifestation of the ten toes and the events that will occur at that time.

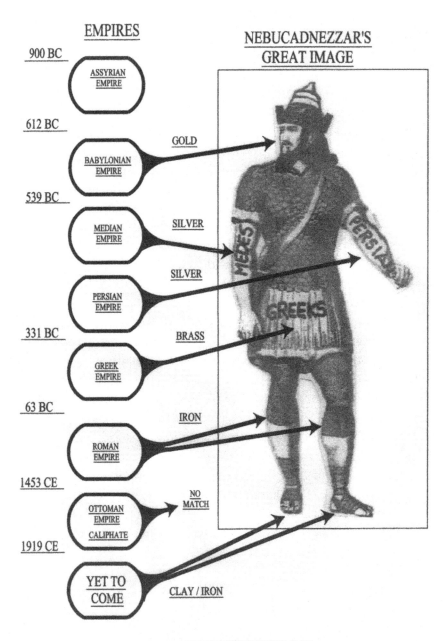

EMPIRES

900 BC

612 BC

539 BC

331 BC

63 BC

1453 CE

1919 CE

ASSYRIAN EMPIRE

BABYLONIAN EMPIRE — GOLD

MEDIAN EMPIRE — SILVER

PERSIAN EMPIRE — SILVER

GREEK EMPIRE — BRASS

ROMAN EMPIRE — IRON

OTTOMAN EMPIRE CALIPHATE — NO MATCH

YET TO COME — CLAY / IRON

NEBUCADNEZZAR'S GREAT IMAGE

MEDES PERSIA GREEKS

HISTORIC TIMELINE OF ANCIENT EMPIRES

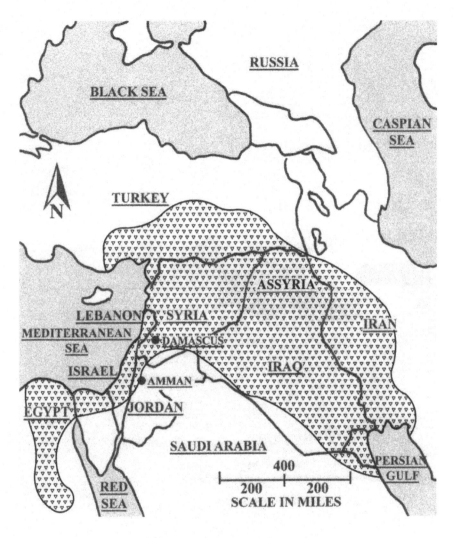

<u>The Assyrian Empire,</u>
circa 612 BC

This empire is mapped because it is the forerunner to Nebuchadnezzar's empire and will be referenced in Revelation 17:10. The empire covered the area commonly known as the fertile crescent, from the Persian Gulf in the east to Israel in the west. The empire extended north into modern-day Turkey and west into Egypt's Nile Valley.

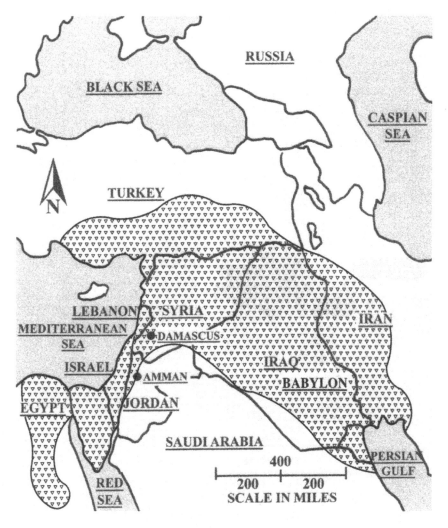

The Babylonian Empire
circa 539 BC

The empire was nearly identical to the Assyrian Empire, which the Babylonians replaced. The empire was enlarged in Turkey and expanded to include the Sinai Peninsula.

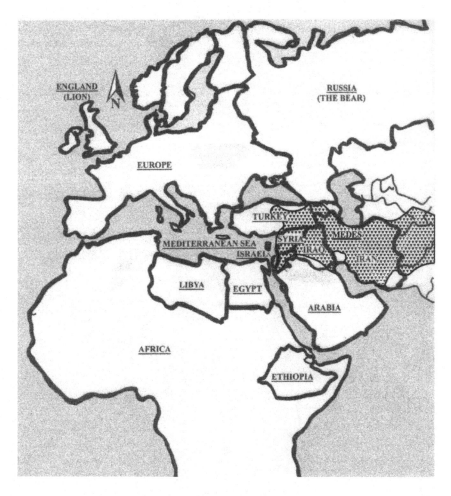

<u>The Median Empire,
replaced the Babylonians in 539 BC</u>

The Medes controlled a much larger area than the
Babylonians. The empire included most of modern-day Iran
and Afghanistan and north to the Caucus Mountains.

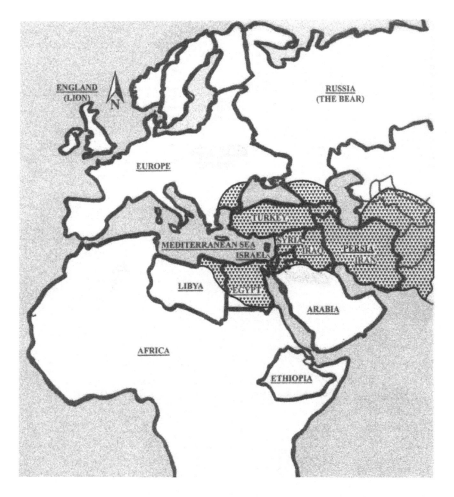

<u>The Persian Empire</u>

circa 331 BC

The Persian Empire was the natural extension of the Medes. The Persians extended the empire into Macedonia in the west, north into Russia, south into Egypt and Libya, and east to India.

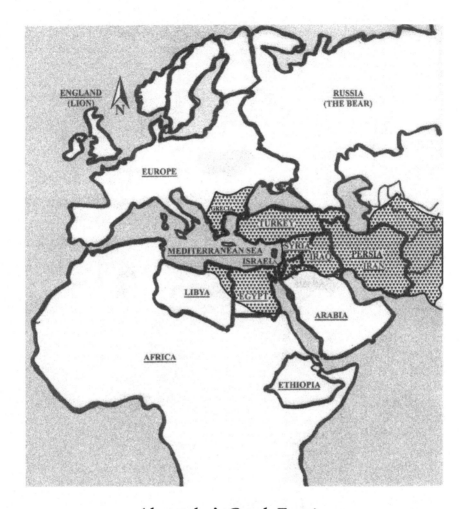

<u>Alexander's Greek Empire</u>
(the Greeks controlled the empire until circa 63 BC)

Alexander's empire replaced the Persian Empire and expanded
to include Grecia in the west. The empire would be divided into
four smaller empires by Alexander's generals after his death.

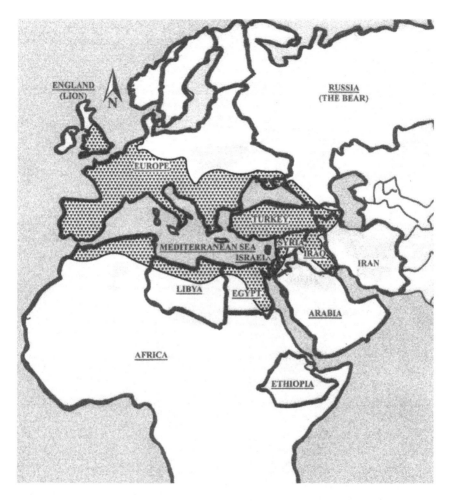

<u>The Roman Empire</u>
63 BC–AD 1458

The Roman Empire controlled the entire coast of the Mediterranean sea. The empire did not extend east as far as the Greeks' empire but did control most of Europe. This is the empire that the final beast's empire will mimic—the two legs, east and west.

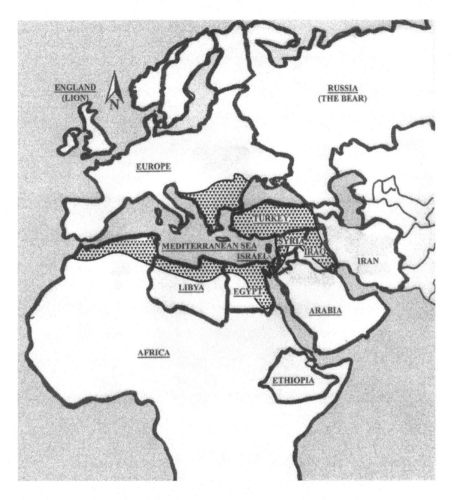

<u>The Ottoman Empire</u>
AD 1458–1919

The Ottoman Empire replaced the Roman Empire by conquering
Constantinople (the Roman's eastern capital). The Ottomans
never controlled the western part of the empire. This empire
did not represent the two feet and ten toes of Daniel 2.

CHAPTER TWO

Daniel 8

Covering this chapter at this point in the study of Daniel would seem out of order, but certain points complement Daniel 2. Daniel 8 shows clearly that the sequence of empires scripturally flows from Babylon to the Medes and Persians and then to the Greeks. It also explains the division of Alexander's Grecian Empire into the subsequent four empires of his generals. It is encouraging for students of biblical prophecy to see the literal fulfilment of the Scriptures; it also helps in interpreting the portions of the visions that still remain to be fulfilled.

> In the third year of the reign of King Belshazzar, a vision appeared unto me, even unto me Daniel, after that which appeared unto me at the first. (2) And I saw in a vision; and it came to pass, when I saw, that I was at Shushan in the palace, which is in the province of Elam; and I saw in a vision, and I was by the river Ulai. (3) Then I lifted up mine eyes, and saw, and, behold, there stood before the river a ram which had two horns: and the two horns were high; but one was higher than the other, and the higher came up last. (4) I saw the ram pushing westward, and northward, and southward; so that no beasts might stand before him, neither was there any that could deliver out of his hand; but he did according to his will, and became great. (5) And as

I was considering, behold, a he-goat came from the west on the face of the whole earth, and touched not the ground: and the goat had a notable horn between his eyes. (6) And he came to the ram that had two horns, which I had there seen standing before the river, and ran unto him in the fury of his power. (7) And I saw him come close unto the ram, and he was moved with choler against him, and smote the ram, and brake his two horns: and there was no power in the ram to stand before him, but he cast him down to the ground and stamped upon him: and there was none that could deliver the ram out of his hand. (8) Therefore the he-goat waxed very great: and when he was strong, the great horn was broken; and for it came up four notable ones toward the four winds of heaven. (Dan. 8:1–8)

At this point in the vision, I want to make some observations. First, we are told that this is the second vision that Daniel was given. (The first vision is found in Daniel 7, which we will study later.) This second vision takes place in the third year of King Belshazzar's reign. Daniel was at the king's palace at Shushan, which is in southeastern Babylon (modern-day Iran); it was then called Elam. While he was physically at the palace, he was at the River Ulai in the vision.

Second, in the vision God begins to show Daniel events, kings, and empires, all represented by animals. The animals that God chooses to use all represent strength and power. Had God chosen to use men in place of the animals, something would have been lost in its effect on Daniel. The animals represent more that just kings; they are empires and whole armies. If you have ever seen two rams colliding in the wild, you know that the impact is incredible—it's hard to believe they can survive such violence. This is what God was trying to convey.

Third, no matter how strong an empire or kingdom might be, it can and will change at some point. The ram is said to be stronger than all the other beasts, and it seems as though the ram's dominance is ensured. But the he-goat takes the ram by surprise. The he-goat is very special indeed; he does not even touch the ground. There are aspects to world events, battles, kings, and nations that go beyond the natural realm into spiritual realities. An example would be the battle of the children of Israel and Amalek, as found in Exodus 17:9–16. When Moses held up his hands, the children of Israel prevailed in the battle, but when his hands dropped, the battle turned. Aaron and Hur stayed Moses's hands, and the battle was won. It is important to never put your trust in natural strength; it is only part of the equation and will not be the deciding factor. Many battles are not decided by numbers, weapons, men, or even technical superiority but rather by intangibles that no one anticipated. Every army wants to enter battle, believing they have the moral and spiritual high ground.

The vision continues:

> (9) And out of one of them came forth a little horn, which waxed exceeding great, toward the south, and toward the east, and toward the pleasant land. (10)And it waxed great, even to the host of heaven; and it cast down some of the host and of the stars to the ground, and stamped upon them. (11) Yea he magnified himself even to the prince of the host, and by him the daily sacrifice was taken away, and the place of his sanctuary was cast down. (12) and a host was given him against the daily sacrifice by reason of transgression, and it cast down the truth to the ground; and it practiced, and prospered.

This small horn that rises from and after the four horns is not seen in Daniel 2, but he is so prominent, it's hard to know why he wasn't, other than to say that Daniel 2 is an overview of the empires, and the account in Daniel 8 adds details not seen before. Since this small horn has never manifested in history, it is reasonable to look for him, like the ten toes, as a future event.

The he-goat with the notable horn is described as "very great" and "strong," but the little horn is described as "exceeding great," and he waxed great even to the host of heaven. The descriptive term "little" must not refer to his power or greatness but to his beginnings or even his stature. He will be greater and stronger than the historic Greek king Alexander the Great (the he-goat).

While the little horn's ambitions may not be any greater than Alexander's, his success will be. His battles will be fought in both the natural realm, using armies, and in the heavenly realm, the spirit. He will fight even to the host of heaven (the armies of God). Scripture states that he has at least some measure of success against God's host:

23

(10) and it [the little horn] cast down some of the host and the stars to the ground.

The reference to stars denotes the angels of God.

The little horn will magnify himself, even to the prince of the host. The prince of the host is the Lord himself, the Lord of hosts. The little horn believes himself to be equal to the Lord of hosts. His arrogance is incredible. He has no regard for truth—he casts it to the ground. He also attempts to halt the worship and sacrifices to God in God's sanctuary:

(11) and by him [the little horn] the daily sacrifice was taken away, and the place of his [God's] sanctuary was cast down.

The little horn is given an army (host) to accomplish his attack on Jerusalem and the sanctuary. He uses this army to attack to the south and east and to the Holy land. Under the command of the little horn, no one could stop this army from accomplishing its tasks and "it practiced and prospered."

These events are yet to happen. The destruction of the temple by the Romans in AD 70 did not happen as described in Daniel. Clearly, the restoration of the Jewish people to their homeland and to the temple mount in Jerusalem is required for this prophecy to be fulfilled. Much has been accomplished toward the fulfillment of this prophecy. The Jewish state of Israel now exists, and Jewish control of Jerusalem has been restored, however the temple mount still is under the control of Islam. Again, we see Islam obstructing the express will of God concerning the Jews, the land of Israel, and the temple mount. A major change is needed in order for a Jewish temple to be built on the mount, much less the subsequent stopping of the daily sacrifice. The Islamic caliphate of the Ottoman Empire refused to relinquish God's land, as given to Moses and the children of Israel. The Ottoman Empire was defeated before the land could return to the Jews. It certainly does not seem likely that current Islamic control of the temple mount will be relinquished to the state of Israel any easier than it was by the Ottomans. We can expect that some sort of military action will lead to the removal of Islamic control; this will be a major world event when it happens. Like the restoration of Jerusalem to Jewish control, which came from a failed military campaign by Israel's neighbors, Israel more likely will be defending itself when the action starts.

The vision continues:

> (13) Then I heard one saint speaking, and another saint said unto that certain saint which spake, How long shall be the vision concerning the daily sacrifice, and the transgression of desolation, to give both the sanctuary and the host to be trodden under foot? (14) And he said unto me, Unto two thousand and three hundred days; then shall the sanctuary be cleaned. (15) And it came to pass, when I, even I Daniel, had seen the vision, and sought for the meaning, then, behold, there stood before me as the appearance of a man. (16) And I heard a man's voice between the banks of Ulai, which called, and said, Gabriel, make this man to understand the vision.

These Scriptures could be used to give this vision a title: the "vision concerning the daily sacrifice and the transgression of desolation." This theme is seen in many of Daniel's prophecies and echoed by Jesus in the Gospels. This event is so central to end-time events that the saints within the vision want to know how long the sanctuary and the host will be trodden under foot. We learn that the duration is not long, especially in terms of prophetic events. When stated in days, it appears to be longer than it actually is. We are told it is twenty-three hundred days—this is six years, four months, and twenty days. At the end of this time, the sanctuary will be cleansed. It is not clear, using just the information found within this vision, exactly when the time will start. This time frame will be studied in more detail from other locations within the book of Daniel. As the vision continues, the angel Gabriel is told to make this man understand the vision.

> (17) So he came near where I stood: and when he came, I was afraid, and fell upon my face: but he said unto me, Understand, O son of man: for at the time of the end shall be the vision. (18) Now as he was speaking with me, I was in a deep sleep on my face toward the ground: but he touched me, and set me upright.

(19) And he said, behold, I will make thee know what shall be in the last of the indignation: for at the time appointed the end shall be. (20) The ram which thou sawest having two horns are the kings of Media and Persia. (21) And the rough goat is the king of Grecia: and the great horn that is between his eyes is the first king. (22) Now that being broken, whereas four stood up for it, four kingdoms shall stand up out of the nation, but not in his power. (23) And in the later time of their kingdom, when the transgressors are come to the full, a king of fierce countenance, and understanding dark sentences, shall stand up. (24) And his power shall be mighty, but not by his own power: and he shall destroy wonderfully, and shall prosper, and practice, and shall destroy the mighty and the holy people. (25) And through his policy also he shall cause craft to prosper in his hand; and he shall magnify himself in his heart, and by peace shall destroy many: he shall also stand up against the Prince of princes; but he shall be broken without hand. (26) And the vision of the evening and the morning which was told is true: wherefore shut thou up the vision; for it shall be for many days. (27) And I Daniel fainted, and was sick certain days; afterward I rose up, and did the king's business; and I was astonished at the vision, but none understood it.

God sends the angel Gabriel to Daniel to give him information concerning the interpretation of the vision; Gabriel comes in the form of a man. Although Gabriel comes as a man, his appearance still greatly affects Daniel. As Gabriel approaches Daniel, Daniel falls on his face in fear. The first thing Gabriel says to Daniel is that the vision is for the time of the end. I suppose the news that the vision is not going to happen soon was meant to calm Daniel, but he continues on his face in a deep sleep. I think Daniel, being a man, although a spiritual man, was still in shock at what he just had seen. This would never do; Gabriel touches him and literally sets Daniel upright.

Gabriel tells Daniel that the vision applies to the "last end of the indignation." The term indignation is the wrath of God that will come to end the world. It also is known as the "day of the Lord," the time that God comes to end the world system and set up his kingdom. We saw reference to that day, as the stone cut out without hands that destroys the sequence of world empires, in Daniel 2. Thus, we know that the little horn is the leader of the ten toes, an alliance of mingled peoples, part clay and part iron—partly strong and partly weak. He is to arise from out of one of the four kingdoms—four horns that survive the great horn of the he-goat, Alexander the Great. Gabriel does not tell us from which kingdom he will come, but we will be able to ascertain that information from later chapters in the book of Daniel.

Gabriel reveals that the ram with two horns is, in fact, the kingdom of the Medes and Persians. The he-goat is the king of Grecia, and when he is broken (dead), his empire will be divided into four empires. The four horns represent four kings, but the kings were not kings to begin with; they were generals. They were military commanders, and each general commanded many different nations. The dividing of Alexander's Greek Empire is seen precisely in history. So precise is the fulfillment of this vision that many history scholars, even some biblical scholars, believe that the book of Daniel must have been written after the events had taken place. They believe the writing of Daniel was done around 160 BC, at the time of the Greek king Antiochus IV. Antiochus fulfilled much of what the little horn would do. He was an incredibly evil man with an intense hatred for God and the Jewish people, but he did not fulfill all that would be required. The end of God's indignation did not come, and the world system is still with us today, two thousand years after Antiochus. We also know from Daniel 2 that the ten toes come after the two iron legs—the Romans—not before. When the disciples of Jesus asked him about the signs of the end of the world and his coming, he stated the following:

> When ye therefore shall see the abomination of desolation, spoken of by Daniel the prophet, stand in the holy place, (whoso readeth, let him understand:) Then let them which be in Judaea flee into the mountains. (Matt. 24:15–16)

Jesus told his disciples to look forward to Daniel's events, not back to Antiochus. The events were still yet to come, some 160 years after Antiochus.

It also should be noted that Jesus did not see the book of Daniel as a forgery written after the fact. He saw it as accurate and authoritative, and he references it for the signs of the end.

Gabriel introduces us to a king who is yet to come; he is a king of fierce countenance who understands dark sentences. His countenance refers to his appearance and, specifically, his face. He will be a man who means business, who is focused on the tasks before him and not someone to be trifled with. This king will have discernment concerning the meanings of obscure riddles. In the spirit realm, much communication is made through symbols and pictures. The communication is not meant for everyone to read but only for the worthy initiate—those who can be trusted with the information. Just being able to read or interpret a dark communication is not enough; one must know the meaning and application. This king will be adept in these areas.

As Daniel had a relationship with the God of heaven, and he knew and interpreted the dreams for Nebuchadnezzar, the source of which was God, this king of fierce countenance will have a relationship with the dark spiritual sources.

The king's power will be great but not from his own power. For those who will see and work with him, the power will appear to be his. He will appear to be very special, in the same way that Hitler appeared special to the German people. But in reality, his power will come from the dark spiritual sources. He will have an alternative source of power, opposite to the God of heaven.

We are told that he will destroy wonderfully. The term "wonderfully" means to use wonders, as in signs, wonders, and miracles. He will use them to spoil and corrupt and ruin many people. He will use them to convince the world that he is the legitimate king of the world.

The timing of the arrival of this king is said to be when the transgressors are come to the full. In the book of Revelation, chapters seventeen and eighteen, we see end-time Babylon coming to the time of judgment, and her sins and transgressions are seen in a cup that she holds. Her cup is full. Like Babylon, the world is filling its cup to the fullest. God's judgment is coming to an unrepentant world, a world ready to receive the dark king.

This king will practice and prosper for a time and will conquer many people through his policy of peace and his ability to cause business to prosper. Because this king desires to rule everyone and believes he is Sharrukin (the legitimate king), the peace policy will be cast aside, and he will challenge all that is of God. He will attempt to destroy all of Israel and the Jewish people. He will be successful up to a point, but in the end, he will be broken (killed). This king will be broken "<u>without hand</u>." I believe this reference is to the stone cut out without hands that is referred to in Daniel 2, which comes to end the world system and set up God's kingdom. The direct intervention by the Messiah (the Prince of princes) will end it all.

<u>Summary of Daniel 8</u>

1. This is the second vision seen by Daniel. He was at the palace in Shushan, in southeastern Babylon (modern-day Iran). The vision is called the "vision concerning the daily sacrifice and the transgression of desolation" (verse 13).

2. The vision identifies seven empires that will come between Babylon and the Roman Empire—the Median and Persian Empires and the five different empires of the Greeks—Alexander and his four generals (verses 20–22).

3. The vision uses a he-goat with one notable horn to represent Alexander's kingdom. When the horn is broken (when he dies), four new horns appear on the he-goat, which represent the four military generals that divide the empire into four. The military commanders each rule over a large area and many nations (verses 8, 22).

4. The vision introduces another horn that will come up from the area of the Greek Empire in the last days. This king will fight against the Prince of princes and will be defeated. He will be broken without hands, not by man but by the Lord of hosts (verses 9, 25).

5. The little horn is powerful—not in his own power but from the dark spiritual forces he uses. He will attack Israel and will prosper and practice for a time, but he ultimately will be stopped by God's intervention. The little horn is arrogant, and he lifts himself up, even to the Lord of hosts (verses 24–25).

6. He will initially use a peace policy to deceive many people into believing he is the right man to rule the world. He believes he is the legitimate king, Sharrukin (verse 25).

7. The little horn is the man who will cause the Jewish daily sacrifices to cease, and he will commit the transgression of desolation, also known

as the abomination of desolation. He will trod down the Jewish temple in Jerusalem, the sanctuary (verses 12–13).

8. The duration of the vision is twenty-three hundred ninety days, or six years, four months, and six days (verse 14).

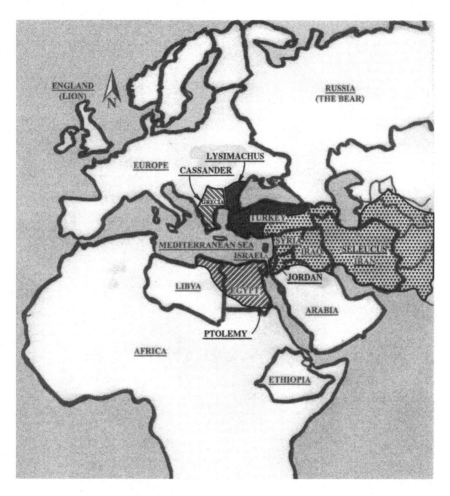

The Grecian Empire after Alexander
(the empire ended in 63 BC)

This map show the four regions of the Grecian Empire after
Alexander—**Cassander**: Grecia; **Lysimachus**: Macedonia
and northern Turkey; **Ptolemy**: Egypt and northeast Libya;
and **Seleucus**: the Middle East and eastward. The Seleucid
Empire is the area from which the little horn will rise.

CHAPTER THREE

Daniel 7

This chapter covers the first dream and vision that Daniel receives from God. The dream comes in the first year of Belshazzar's reign and uses animals to represent the empires that lead the world into the establishment of God's kingdom at the end of days. The little horn also is seen in the vision, and we are given more information to understand him and his empire.

(1) In the first year of Belshazzar, king of Babylon, Daniel had a dream and visions of his head upon his bed: then he wrote the dream, and told the sum of the matters. (2) Daniel spake and said, I saw in my vision by night, and behold, the four winds of the heaven strove upon the great sea. (3) And four great beasts came up from the sea, diverse one from another. (4) The first was like a lion, and had eagle's wings: I beheld till the wings thereof were plucked, and it lifted up from the earth, and made stand upon the feet as a man, and a man's heart was given to it. (5) And behold another beast, a second, like to a bear, and it raised up itself on one side, and it had three ribs in the mouth of it between the teeth of it: and they said unto it, Arise, devour much flesh. (6) After this I beheld, and lo another, like a leopard, which had upon the back of it four wings of a fowl; the beast had also four heads; and dominion was given to it. (7) After this I saw in the night visions, behold a fourth beast,

dreadful and terrible, and strong exceedingly; and it had great iron teeth: it devoured and brake in pieces, and stamped the residue with the feet of it: and it was diverse from all the beasts that were before it; and it had ten horns. (8) I considered the horns, and behold, there came up among them another little horn, before whom there were three of the first horns plucked up by the roots and, behold in this horn were eyes like the eyes of man, and a mouth speaking great things.

The basic outline of the four animals and empires is as follows: The first is a lion with eagle's wings. The lion has a lion's heart, because when this empire begins to wane, the lion will be given the heart of a man. It also will be made to stand upright like a man and will cease moving like a lion. The wings, which also represent movement, will be plucked so that they no longer can be used. It must be noted that this kingdom will not be destroyed but simply will be forced to yield its dominion to others. This is seen in verse 12.

(12) ...They had their dominion taken away: yet their lives were prolonged for a season.

The second animal is a bear, with all the attributes you would expect from a bear. This empire will be brutal. It will be very strong militarily and will devour much flesh. The empire will arise from outside the great sea area and will insert its influence into the Middle East. It will rise up on one side. The bear also will lose its dominion but keep its life for a season.

The third animal is like a leopard, with four wings on its back and four heads. This is one empire, but it has many different aspects, such as the four heads, which could mean four different yet simultaneous leaders. It could represent four different nations making up the empire, or the four wings could mean that the empire is spread out over a large area. This empire also will lose its dominion but will continue for a season. The descriptions given for these empires are not complete to the point that we can identify them just from this vision.

After Daniel sees the first three beasts, he beholds a fourth beast come up. This beast is different from the other three beasts—it comes up from a different location. There will be aspects of this beast that make it different and separate it from the other beasts. This beast is exceedingly strong and has great iron teeth. Just like the bear, it devours. It also breaks in pieces and stamps what is left over with its feet. This beast is the most powerful empire to have existed. This empire has great military assets and is willing to use them. The empire is actually very brutal. It does not just defeat its enemies; it destroys them, and once they are down, it stamps them out. The actions of an empire will reflect the attitude and personality of its leader. This empire shows an attitude of extreme anger. Something is wrong with its leadership.

Daniel sees the fourth empire as having ten horns. As Daniel considers the horns, another little horn emerges. This new, eleventh horn has eyes, like the eyes of a man, and a mouth that makes great statements and says things that get everyone's attention. It seems he will not come to power by force but rather politically and through his policies and speeches. However, at some point in time he will be in the position to pluck up three of the original horns by the roots. This shows that he is not all talk and no action; when given the opportunity, he will be brutal. We know that the little horn of Daniel 8 initially conquers through a policy of peace, only to later turn violent, even to the point of fighting God.

Daniel watches until he sees the spiritual powers of this world cast down. This was done by the Ancient of days, whose garment was white as snow, and the hair of his head like pure wool. His throne was like the fiery flame, and his wheels like burning fire.

The vision continues in Daniel 7:

> (9) I beheld till the thrones were cast down, and the Ancient of days did sit, whose garment was white as snow, and the hair of his head like the pure wool: his throne was like the fiery flame, and his wheels as the burning fire. (10) A fiery stream issued and came forth from before him: thousand thousands ministered unto him, and ten thousand times ten thousand stood before him: the judgment was set, and the books were opened. (11) I beheld then because of the voice of the great words which the horn spake: I beheld even till the beast was slain, and his body destroyed, and given to the burning flame.(12) As concerning

the rest of the beasts, they had their dominion taken away: yet their lives were prolonged for a season and a time.

Daniel continued to watch the developments until the end, when the thrones were cast down. The thrones refers to the high spiritual powers of darkness. We see this explained in Colossians 1:16:

> For by him were all things created, that are in heaven, and that are in earth, visible and invisible, whether they be thrones, or dominions, or principalities, or powers.

And we see it again in Ephesians 6:12:

> For we wrestle not against flesh and blood, but against principalities, against powers, against rulers of the darkness of this world, against spiritual wickedness in high places.

We saw that the little horn was adept in understanding dark sentences and communicating with the spiritual darkness. Now we see that his demise and the judgment of the rulers of darkness are connected and will happen during the same time. We also see that the judgment comes from the Ancient of days as he sits on his throne, a throne of fire. We also see that God is attended by an incredible number of ministers—ten thousand times ten thousand stand before him. What an incredible sight Daniel sees. John saw the same event and recorded it in Revelation 20:11–12:

> And I saw a great white throne, and him that sat on it, from whose face the earth and the heaven fled away: and there was found no place for them. (12) And I saw the dead, small and great, stand before God, and the books were opened.

The vision continues in Daniel 7:

> (13) I saw in the night visions, and, behold, one like the Son of man came with the clouds of heaven, and came to the Ancient of days, and they brought him before him. (14) And there

was given him dominion, and glory, and a kingdom, that <u>all</u> <u>people, nations, and languages</u>, should serve him: his dominion is an everlasting dominion, which shall not pass away, and his kingdom that which shall not be destroyed.

The term "Son of man" is used extensively in the New Testament to describe Jesus as the Messiah. An example would be Matthew 24:30:

And then shall appear the sign of the <u>Son of man</u> in <u>heaven</u>: and then shall all the tribes of the earth mourn, and <u>they shall</u> <u>see</u> the <u>Son of man</u> coming in the <u>clouds of heaven</u> with power and great glory.

It seems clear that the events that Daniel describes at the end of his vision are going to be manifested to the nations (the "tribes") of the world at the time of the end. The end of Daniel's vision applies to the time when God—the Ancient of days, the God of heaven—will set up his kingdom, and he uses the Prince of princes, the Son of man, to accomplish the task.

The vision continues in Daniel 7:

(15) I Daniel was grieved in my spirit in the midst of my body, and the visions of my head troubled me. (16) I came near unto one of them that stood by, and asked him the truth of all this. So he told me, and made me know the interpretation of the things. (17) These great beasts, which are four, are four kings, which shall arise out of the earth. (18) But the saints of the most High shall take the kingdom, and possess the kingdom for ever, even for ever and ever. (19) Then I would know the truth of the fourth beast, which was diverse from all the others, exceeding dreadful, whose teeth were of iron, and his nails of brass; which devoured, brake in pieces, and stamped the residue with his feet; (20) And of the ten horns that were in his head, and of the other which came up, and before whom three fell; even of that horn that had eyes, and the mouth that spake very great things, whose look was more stout than his fellows.

Daniel is grieved by all the things he witnesses in the vision, and he is truly disturbed by what is going to happen. But in spite of his feelings, he still wants to know what it all means, even to the point of asking someone nearby what the truth of all this is. We are not told to whom Daniel speaks, only that he obliges Daniel, and tells him the interpretation. The interpretation given only speaks in general terms about the four beasts being kings (kingdoms) and that the end is the kingdom that shall last forever. This is not good enough for Daniel. He wants to know more about the fourth beast—the ten horns and the little horn—whose look was stouter than his fellows. It seems clear that Daniel felt that the ten horns and the little horn was the most important aspect of the vision.

The interpretation continues:

> (21)I beheld, and the same horn made war with the saints, and prevailed against them; (22) Until the Ancient of days came, and judgment was given to the saints of the most High; and the time came that the saints possessed the kingdom. (23) Thus he said, The fourth beast shall be the fourth kingdom upon earth, which shall be diverse from all kingdoms, and shall devour the whole earth, and shall tread it down, and break it in pieces. (24) And the ten horns out of his kingdom are ten kings that shall arise: and another shall rise after them; and he shall be diverse from the first, and shall subdue three kings, (25) And he shall speak great words against the most High, and shall wear out the saints of the most High, and think to change times and laws: and they shall be given into his hand until a time and times and a dividing of time. (26) But the judgment shall sit, and they shall take away his dominion, to consume and to destroy it unto the end.

The little horn will hate God's people and war against them. He will have success up to a point and for a short time. The little horn actually will control, or devour, the whole earth, and the extent of the damage and mayhem he will creates will be astounding. The horn will wear out the saints; his pressure against them will be relentless, and it will take a toll. The saints will not defeat the little horn through their own strength or any special manifestation through them. God will allow him to prevail until the Ancient of days comes to take the kingdom, and he gives it to the saints.

The fourth beast is completely new and different from all previous empires. It will come up from and control the old Roman Empire—both legs, east and west. But its structure will be new and unique. The old empires in history were centered around a single nation, which became very strong and aggressive and extended its influence into many of the neighboring nations. These empires generally expanded until they no longer have the resources to maintain control or until the leadership weakens.

The fourth empire has no central nation, but it appears to have ten leaders controlling many peoples, or nations. These leaders appear to share power until the little horn, speaking great things, talks them into allowing him to run the show. At some point later in his reign, he will pluck up, or destroy three of the original horns. It's clear that he is not to be trifled with. Earlier in this chapter, I explained that something was wrong with the leadership of this kingdom. It is the little horn. He completely rebels against God and exalts himself against God. This anger is seen in the attitude of his empire. He is so arrogant that during the time he is in control, he begins to change times and laws. He wants the world to reflect his values and his ways; he wants to cast down all that pertains to the God of heaven. God allows him to trample underfoot the people and the sanctuary for a "time and times and a dividing of time." The term "time," as used in this account, is understood to be a year. Thus, his control is for one year (time) plus two years (times) and a half year (a dividing of time), for a total of three and one-half years. In verse 26 we are assured that God's judgment will stand and is unalterable; the little horn's dominion will be taken away, and he will no longer consume and destroy.

The vision comes to an end:

> (27) And the kingdom and dominion, and the greatness of the kingdom under the whole heaven, shall be given to the people of the saints of the most High, whose kingdom is an everlasting kingdom, and all dominions shall serve and obey him. (28) Hitherto is the end of the matter. As for me Daniel,

my cogitations much troubled me, and my countenance changed in me: but I kept the matter in my heart.

For Daniel's vision, this is the end of the matter. It is the end of the world and the world's empires. The tribes and nations of the world will be required to serve and obey God and live under the rule of the Son of man and saints of God to whom the kingdom is given.

Contemporary Fulfillment of Daniel 7

In Daniel 2, we found a series of empires that end with the two feet and ten toes. This last empire will be destroyed by the stone cut out without hands. This event will allow for the kingdom of God to come. So we now are waiting for the two feet and ten toes, with the ten toes being the last to be seen. The ten toes are the equivalent to the ten horns of Daniel 7, because they exist at the same point in time, just prior to the Son of man. This being the case, we know that the lion, bear, and leopard will exist sequentially, before the ten horns. We also know that the Islamic caliphate of the Ottomans disrupted the historic sequence of empires, but with the Ottoman Empire's defeat in World War I, the way was made clear for the prophetic events to resume. In fact, the next empire to control the land of Israel and Jerusalem is the British Empire.

The British Lion

The British Empire became the protectorate of Israel and Jerusalem in 1920, immediately after World War I. The British Empire has been symbolized by the lion and known as the lion-hearted. The British Empire now has been plucked of most of its colonies and certainly of all its control in the Middle East. England, having lost its empire, has not lost much of its global influence. The English language still is used extensively throughout the world, and London is a center of trade and finances for global markets. Britain is still a nuclear power and ranks fifth in the world in military power, behind the USA, China, Russia, and India. Yet at the height of British power, England and her colonies were able to stand toe-to-toe against Germany and Hitler's military might. In 1948, England walked away from Palestine and left the fledgling Jewish nation of Israel to fend for itself against her Arab neighbors, who were waiting to drive the Jews into the sea and reclaim the land for Islam. Israel won the wars, and England lost its empire.

The Russian Bear

When the Israelis won their independence from their Arab neighbors, their Arab neighbors needed to restore their forces. Egypt, Syria, and Jordan all needed assistance to fund and rebuild their military structure, so they turned to the Soviet Union for help. The Soviet Union was a Russian-led empire that had a hatred for Israel and Israel's biggest supporter, the United States. The Russian bear was more than willing to throw its power and resources behind Israel's enemies. They supplied weapons, weapon systems, training, and funding to see Israel eliminated. From 1948 through to about 1991, the Soviet Union did all that it could, through its surrogates, to destroy Israel. After several additional Middle East wars, the Israelis established their nation and were victorious. Russia did not succeed in destroying the nation of Israel.

The Soviet Union was known for its brutality, especially when it came to keeping control of its people and the multitude of different ethnic groups found within its huge Asian land mass. The government was officially an atheistic system. No religion was supported, and no religion was safe; the government put all religious groups under subjection, including Islam.

The Soviet Union collapsed in the mid-1990s from economic pressures and failures of the socialist system. Many of the nations held under Soviet control received their independence, and the Soviet-controlled Warsaw Pact alliance fell apart. Aid and support for the Arab causes against Israel also ceased. The Palestinian Liberation Organization—designed, operated, and funded by the Soviets—had to change. It had to take on a new direction and a new name, becoming the Palestinian Authority and marking the change in Middle East authority.

Russia, like England, has lost most of its influence and empire. It still exists, like a bear in hibernation, but it is a shadow of its past strength. Russia, however, is still a nuclear power and ranks third in military power in the world today, just behind the USA and China.

The Islamic Leopard

How do we define the current Middle East power structure? I think that after the fall of the Soviet Union, the power structure of the Arab nations initially was in the hands of independent leaders, with strong-arm governments. But with the Iranian revolution in 1979, a trend began. The Islamic clergy never has been satisfied with the non-Islamic governments found in the Middle East, in general. The clergy believes that Moslem adherents throughout the world should not be subject to non-Islamic governments and laws. Just having Moslems in leadership positions within a nation does not make the government Islamic. The Islamic clergy would have every Moslem living under sharia law; anything short of this is an unsatisfactory compromise. This goal of sharia law domination has not been realized but was closest during the Ottoman Empire.

During the Iranian revolution in 1979, the West used the term "fundamentalist Moslems" to describe the movement and the revolution. This came from the view that the Iranian Islamic clergy simply was trying to return to a more fundamental or pious form of Islam—back to the their core values. The Iranian form of Islam is Shia. The Shiite Moslems are a minority in the Moslem world, and it is unlikely that the movement would spread beyond the Iranian borders.

Iranian fundamentalism has spread beyond Iran and has attacked the infidels in Europe, the United States, and Russia. They have gone from being known as fundamentalists to being called fanatics, militant Islam, Islamic extremists, and terrorists. The movement to spread sharia law has been instrumental in the fall of several nations with Moslem majorities, such as Egypt, Tunisia, and Libya. Uprisings in these nations grew out of the people's extreme exasperation and their desire for a better life. Groups like the Moslem Brotherhood, however, are better organized than the grassroots movements and are able to greatly influence the situation and take control. The internal struggles in these countries have not been resolved and could become very violent. The minority religions within these nations already have felt the negative impact—persecution. Several other nations, including Syria and Yemen, are under assault, and their governments are likely to fall.

The movement of turning to sharia law and clerical rule within the Moslem nations of the world could result in a **new Islamic caliphate** being pushed forward from Iran (formerly Persia) and those nations that support Iran. The term *caliphate* refers to an **Islamic empire.**

The establishment of any empire requires time and patience to develop to its final form. It isn't established overnight, and it doesn't completely end overnight. The scriptural description and revelation of this Islamic caliphate—"the nation of Islam," with its wings and heads—will become clearer in the near future. The extent of Islamic influence in the Middle East and the world at large can be seen when looking at the map on page xx.

The Western world is now becoming aware of the Islamic threat and is struggling with how to fight and defeat it. Russia learned from its foray into Afghanistan in the 1980s that no one nation alone, no matter how powerful, can defeat terrorism. It will take a strong, determined effort by many nations to break the back of this caliphate. It will take the same kind of effort as was put forth to defeat the Ottomans in World War I. The framework for the replacement of the caliphate already is forming and will rise from within the old Roman Empire.

Some believe that the European Union (EU) will be the framework that evolves into the ten-horned beast. While I understand the reasoning for this belief and have looked into it very seriously, I find it very unlikely that the EU will become the beast. First, the EU is an economic union, not a military one. While economics play a large part in the beast's empire, the beast's empire primarily will be a military entity. The EU is designed to compete economically with the United States and China by combining the economic power of the European nations. The introduction of the euro as the universal European currency was designed to promote European economic unity and bring about a sort of "United States of Europe." Second, the expansion of the EU outside Europe—to northern Africa, the Middle East, and Asia—would not help to concentrate economic power in Europe. The two legs of the Roman Empire, the east and west, requires the beast to be much more than a European economic union; it must include parts of Asia, Africa and the Middle East. (See map on page xx.)

There is, however, an organization already in existence that fits the scriptural requirements and which already has begun to function in its role to end the rising nation of Islam.

FOUR GREAT BEASTS FROM THE SEA

LION

- WINGS LIKE AN EAGLE
- WINGS WERE PLUCKED
- GIVEN A MAN'S HEART
- MADE TO STAND LIKE A MAN
- CONTINUES TO LIVE AFTER FINAL KINGDOM IS DESTROYED

BEAR

- RISES UP FROM ONE SIDE
- THREE RIBS IN THE MOUTH
- TOLD TO DEVOUR MUCH FLESH
- CONTINUES TO LIVE AFTER FINAL KINGDOM IS DESTROYED

LEOPARD

- FOUR WINGS OF A FOWL
- IT HAS FOUR HEADS
- IT IS GIVEN DOMINION
- CONTINUES TO LIVE AFTER FINAL KINGDOM IS DESTROYED

TEN HORNS

- DREADFUL / TERRIBLE AND STRONG EXCEEDINGLY
- IT HAS IRON TEETH
- IT IS DIVERSE FROM THE OTHER BEASTS
- A SMALL HORN RISES FROM AMONG THE TEN HORNS
- LITTLE HORN LOSSES DOMINION
- GOD'S EVERLASTING KINGDOM COMES
- THE END OF THE MATTER

ARRANGEMENT OF DANIEL CHAPTER SEVEN

The NATO Alliance
and Its Transformation

The North Atlantic Treaty Organization (NATO) was formed in 1949 to—in scriptural terms—protect the lion from the bear. After World War II, the Soviet Union was threatening to attack into western Europe, and no one nation in Europe could stop Russia from doing so. The Western European nations were in desperate need of rebuilding and a general recovery. The United States and Canada were two nations that came out of the war stronger and wealthier than before. A lack of cohesive military alliances before the war was one of the reasons Hitler was so territorially successful.

The NATO alliance was born from this post-war situation. There was nothing sinister in NATO's formation or operations. While it has not always been smooth, the alliance, overall, has performed its mandate of protecting Western Europe. With the wealth and military commitment of the United States, NATO had a well-defined and well-executed defensive plan.

NATO began with twelve members: Belgium, the Netherlands, Luxembourg, France, the United Kingdom, Canada, Portugal, Italy, Norway, Denmark, Iceland, and the United States. These twelve members agreed that an attack on any one of them would be an attack on all. This doctrine is intact today and has been exercised only once in alliance history—after the attack on the World Trade Center in New York in 2001.

In 1952, Greece and Turkey joined the alliance, followed in 1955 by West Germany. The addition of these nations to the alliance prompted the Soviet Union to form the Warsaw Pact alliance. NATO versus the Warsaw Pact created the front line of what has been called the Cold War.

In 1982, during the Cold War, Spain became a member of NATO. After the breakup of the Soviet Union and the Warsaw Pact in the 1990s, many Eastern European and Balkan nations were accepted as members, bringing NATO's membership total to twenty-eight. NATO has changed from its original defensive intent to one that is much more offensive.

Beyond the current membership, NATO is reaching to many nations outside of Europe. NATO has established programs to develop new NATO member nations, such as the partnership programs and the Mediterranean Dialogue program. NATO developed a special relationship with Russia in 2002, called the NATO Russia Council (NRC). One of the professed goals of the NRC is to jointly fight terrorism.

At the time of this writing, there are twenty-two partner nations (including Russia), seven Mediterranean Dialogue countries, four Istanbul Cooperation Initiative nations, and seven global partners. When you look at a map of NATO and its partners, it becomes clear just how extensive NATO's influence is and how ambitious its plans are. With the two exceptions of the North Atlantic and the global partners, which are outside the old Roman Empire, NATO covers the two legs of Daniel 2 almost perfectly. Eventually, Iran will need to be incorporated into NATO, and this will require the fall of the Islamic caliphate. Between the Mediterranean Dialogue nations—Algeria, Egypt, Jordan, Mauritania, Morocco, and Israel—and the Istanbul Cooperation Initiative nations—Bahrain, Qatar, Kuwait, and the United Arab Emirates—NATO is having a dialogue with most of the eastern Roman Empire. (See NATO map on page 50.)

An interesting development within NATO was the move from its being an American-dominated alliance to its developing the European Security and Defense Identity, or ESDI. The ESDI is a NATO term for "European Security and Defense Identity" (ref. NATO's final report on the project "Development of the European security and defense identity" 2001). Before the end of the Cold War, it was imperative that the United States carry most of the monetary and military load, but without a perceived threat from Russia—indeed, with Russia as a partner—the need for America is diminished. Essentially, Europe wants to control its own defense. The biggest hindrance to this move is the economic commitment required by the Europeans; they have grown accustomed to American support. The United States also has expressed dissatisfaction with the current economic and deployment situation. It is likely that NATO's name will be changed in the future to something more appropriate, such as the Atlantic Pacific Alliance or the Eurasian Alliance.

The structure of the NATO during the Cold War was very different than NATO's structure today. It was much easier to understand the enemy and the battlefield requirements when the Warsaw Pact was in place. The threats to NATO today are much different; they come from the Middle East, from militant Islam, and they are more difficult to define. NATO has redesigned its command system through a program called NATO Transformation; as yet, this transformation has not been completed. NATO used a system of "consensus" to discuss problems and policy; it did not vote on policy. I believe this system will be discarded for all but general policy issues. When it comes to military and tactical decisions, a much more dynamic and flexible system is required. It also has to cross ethnic and religious lines. Often, there is not time to assemble all the members and debate actions and polices. The 2011 NATO operation in Libya was stymied because the Moslem members and the neighboring Moslem nations did not trust an American- and European-led NATO to conduct the operation. It was suggested within NATO that a command group with European and Arab or Moslem commanders be assembled. The nations of Qatar, Turkey, Jordan, and the United Arab Emirates joined NATO's command of the campaign in Libya. The need to further adapt NATO command to an east/west streamlined system is needed. If indeed NATO is the foundation for the ten-horned military empire of Daniel 7, then it would appear that NATO's ultimate transformation would be five commanders from the West and five from the East—the ten toes or ten horns. These horns or toes would transcend national boundaries and conduct military operations. The idea that the horns are commanders and not traditional kings comes from Revelation 17:12:

> And the horns which thou sawest are ten kings, which have received <u>no kingdom</u> as yet: but receive <u>power as kings</u> one hour with the beast.

The term kings, as used in this Scripture also can mean "commander". These kings don't have kingdoms; they only have authority or power <u>as</u> kings. They can command or conduct war but don't have a kingdom to rule. I believe they are a command system of generals over the empire. It can be noted that Alexander the Great's four generals, who acted as kings over the divided empire, were seen as four <u>horns</u> on the beast.

One of the most profound changes to come from the NATO transformation is from a purely defensive alliance to having a very definite offensive direction. This is seen in the NATO term, "out of area operations." This means military operations outside the current membership area. If deemed necessary, NATO can strike other nations. This offensive posture is not just a threat; it is being applied in both Libya and Afghanistan. NATO has developed an army—and the needed assets to use it—called the International Security Assistance Force ("ISAF" (Information about ISAF can be found at isaf.nato.int/leadership.html.) It also should be noted that NATO has a nuclear capability through both the United Kingdom and France.

I will develop NATO's connection with the little horn in later chapters of this book, after I cover more scriptural information.

Summary of Daniel 7

1. The vision came to Daniel in the first year of King Belshazzar's reign (verse 1).

2. Daniel sees four beasts come up from the great sea (Mediterranean Sea), each different from the other (verse 3).

3. The first three beasts are represented by animals—first, a lion; second, a bear; and third, a leopard. The fourth is just a beast with ten horns. It is dreadful, terrible, and exceedingly strong but with no animal comparison (verses 4–7).

4. The first three beasts rise and lose their dominion in sequence but continue to live beyond the dominion and destruction of the fourth beast (verse 12).

5. Another horn—a little horn—comes up among the ten horns of the fourth beast. The little horn is a man who takes control of the fourth beast and conquers the whole earth (verses 8, 18–23).

6. The Ancient of days will destroy the fourth beast, the little horn, and will cast down the spiritual powers of darkness (verse 9).

7. God will set up an everlasting kingdom on earth, through the Son of man, the Messiah, after the fourth beast is destroyed. He will give it to the saints to administer (verses 13, 18, 27).

8. The little horn will trample underfoot the people and the sanctuary for three and one-half years—time, times, and a dividing of time (verse 25).

9. After the Ottoman Empire fell in 1919, the next empire to rule in Israel and Jerusalem was the British Empire, the lion.

10. The next empire in the Middle East after the British lion was the Russian bear.

11. The next power in the Middle East was the rise of the nation of Islam, a caliphate centered from Iran.

12. NATO rose out of the old Roman Empire to fight against Islamic terrorism. To understand and verify statements from this chapter concerning NATO, see nato.int/html.

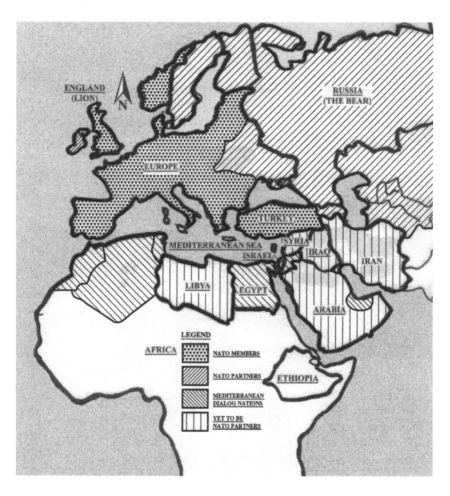

NATO Members and Partners

CHAPTER FOUR

Daniel 11

This chapter covers the events that will befall Daniel's people in the latter days and the four Persian kings that also will rise in those later times. Daniel 10 tells us that a messenger is sent from God to Daniel as an answer to Daniel's prayer and fasting.

> Now I am come to make thee <u>understand what shall befall thy people in the latter days</u> for yet the vision is for many days. (10:14)

It is important for us to understand the intent of the vision. It is meant to inform us concerning the Jewish people in the latter days, not in the time of Daniel. So these future event are recorded by Daniel for future generations to read and understand. The vision itself was revealed to Daniel in the third year of Cyrus, king of Persia.

> Also I [the messenger] in the first year of Darius the Mede, even I [the messenger], stood to confirm and to strengthen him [Darius]. (2) And now will I shew thee [Daniel] the truth. Behold there shall stand up yet three kings in Persia, and the fourth shall be far richer than they all, and by his strength through his riches he shall stir up all against the realm of Grecia. (11:1-2)

A detailed series of events for three of the Persian kings mentioned in verse two is given in verses 3–20. There are those who believe that they can make case for identifing these kings historically, starting with Alexander the Great and ending with Antiochus IV; being the fourth king. We will see from scripture that the fourth Persian king will pollute the sanctuary, take away the daily sacrifice and place the Abomination that maketh desolate. While Antiochus was a truly evil man, and defiled the temple, Jesus taught, some 160 year after Antiochus, that the placing of the Abomination of desolation was yet a future event. In fact Jesus taught that it would be a sign of the end of the age. Matthew 24:15,16.

If the fourth king is not Antiochus IV, then it also is possible that the historic identification of the first three kings is incorrect. The first three kings may be yet to come. The third king is said to be a raiser of taxes from the wealth of the nation, yet we are told he will be destroyed within a few days of coming to power. It is interesting that he only reigns for a few days yet has a reputaion for being a taxer. It suggests that his reputation preceded him. In the old empires, the king would have the power to raise taxes but would not have that authorty before becoming king. It appears that this king may have been operating in a government that delegated the authority of taxation to a body of legislators, or parliament, and recieved his reputation during this time. Persia is the modern-day nation of Iran and currently has an Islamic republic, complete with the appropriate parliament and commitees for the purposes of taxation. It behooves us to watch and study the events in Iran to see what happens. These three leaders could rise and be replaced in a short space of time. Much of what goes on politically in Iran is not made public, so we may not know exactly what is happening.

Because I wish to remain focused on the events of the end of the age, I will deal only with the fourth king and the identifing information given.

> And in his [the third king's] estate shall stand up a vile person [the fourth king], to whom they shall not give the honour of the kingdom, but he shall come in peacebly, and obtain the kingdom by flatteries. (22) And with the arms of a flood shall they be overflown from before him,and shall be broken, yea, also the prince of the covenant. (11:21)

We are told that this man is vile, which means a morally abhorrent person. This is not a good way to be described by God. Those within the nation of Persia who have the authority to establish the next king refused to accept this man as king, but he did not give up. He campaigned through flatteries and politics to talk his way into office. He used a policy of peace to convince some to support him. Ultimately, he raised an army (arms) to take the nation by force. He also fights against a person called the prince of the covenant. This person simply may have be the head of the Persian confederacy at that time, or it might be a reference to the prince of the holy covenant and the vile man's rebellion against God. Either way, the stage is set.

> (23) And after the league made with him he shall work deceitfully: for he shall come up, and shall become strong with a small people. (24) He shall enter peaceably, even upon the fattest places of the province; and he shall do that which his fathers have not done, nor his fathers' fathers; he shall scatter among them the prey, and spoil, and riches: yea, and he will forecast his devices against the strong holds, even for a time.

This king, with all his flatteries, made a lot of promises, but he immediately will begin to work deceitfully behind the scenes—after all, he is a vile man. He will receive much of his support from a small "people" (meaning nation). This king will rise from within one of the many minority peoples in Persia. Persia refers to modern-day Iran, and Iran has many minority peoples. Many of these minorities would not be deemed suitable by the Islamic republic to be a leader today (they would not be honored with the kingdom).

Once he is in power, he will begin to take the wealth of the nation—possibly the taxes raised by his predecessor—and disperse it among the people. This is a shrewd policy. He would gain the support of the population over the old ruling class of his predecessors. We are told that he did that, which his father and his father's father did not do. To the people of Persia, he was a different kind of leader.

The term "forecast his devices" means to cast spells. He will cast these spells against strongholds. The strongholds would be the places and institutions of power controlled by his enemies. This also shows that he is a man who knows and understands the spiritual aspects of leadership. Because he is a vile, morally corrupt person, he will deal with the dark spiritual powers. Nothing godly will come of it.

> (25) And he shall stir up his power and his courage against the king of the south with a great army; and the king of the south shall be stirred up to battle with a very great and mighty army; but he [king of the south] shall not stand: for they shall forecast devices against him. (26) Yea, they that feed of the portion of his meat shall destroy him, and his army shall overflow: and many shall fall down slain.(27) And both these king's hearts shall be to do mischief, and they shall speak lies at one table, but it shall not prosper, for yet the end shall be at the time appointed.

These Scriptures speak of a conflict between the fourth king and the king of the south. The king of the south is believed to be Egypt. Both kings have large, powerful armies, but the Egyptian leader has a weakness within his leadership, they which feed of his meat. The Persian king needs to stir up his courage and his armies, because this is the first time he will move beyond his own borders. The battle is bloody; many are killed. It appears that these two kings attempted to negotiate a settlement to their dispute, but it was doomed to failure, because both men have mischief in their hearts and lied to each other. They had no intention of honoring their word and would strike as soon as possible.

Such a situation is not uncommon. There have been times when a nation used a treaty to lull an enemy into a false sense of safety. Adolf Hitler and the Munich Agreement, signed in 1938, just before World War II, is an example.

> (28) Then shall he [the fourth king] return into his land with great riches: and his heart shall be against the holy covenant; and he shall do exploits, and return to his own land. (29) At the time appointed he shall return, and come toward the south; but it shall not be as the former, or as the latter. (30) For the ships of Chittim shall come against him; therefore, he shall be grieved, and return, and have indignation against the holy covenant:

so shall he do; he shall even return, and have intelligence with them that forsake the holy covenant (31) And arms [armies] shall stand on his part, and they shall pollute the sanctuary of strength, and [he] shall take away the daily sacrifice, and they shall place the abomination that maketh desolate.

After having a successful campaign and removing the plunder and anything he wants from Egypt, he returns home, but something happens in his heart. He lifts himself against the holy covenant. Only God knows what is in the heart of a man, and we are told that this is the point in time when he turns against God and the covenant that God has with his people. The king decides to turn against Israel and Jerusalem. We are told he returns to the south—not Egypt but the holy land. But something amazing happens. A navy from the western isles comes against him, and he has to retreat. A place called Chittim has a navy that is powerful enough to stop the land attack of a large, powerful army. This navy has come to protect Israel and the Jewish people.

In trying to identify who this navy is, we must consider which nations have navies that could conduct such an operation. I believe there are only a handful of nations to consider—the British Royal Navy, the French navy, the Russians, and the Americans. Of these choices, only one has shown the inclination to support Israel—the United States.

The king is grieved and angry and returns home. We are told that he has intelligence with those who have forsaken the holy covenant. The term intelligence in this context means to instruct and to come to an understanding. The nations that have forsaken the holy covenant would be nations that backslid from their Judeo-Christian traditions. These backslidden nations would be from Europe and probably would include Russia. Russia is the mother country of the Russian Orthodox Church. These nations, with an agreement with the fourth king, will turn against and remove the threat of Chittim. We are told that arms will stand on his part—additional forces or armies will support him, and he will be able to go directly to the sanctuary on the temple mount in Jerusalem. He will take away the daily sacrifice and place the abomination of desolation. Jesus refers to this event in the Gospels, when he warns those who are in Judea, "When you see Jerusalem surrounded by armies, flee to the mountains" (Luke 21:20). And he also connects the abomination of desolation, of which the prophet Daniel spoke, to the need to flee to the mountains (Matthew 24:15–16).

The reference to the ships of Chittim is found not only in Daniel 11 but also in Numbers 24. Since Daniel's account applies to the vile king of the end-times and his affect on Daniel's people, it is worth the effort to look into the Numbers account. The Numbers account comes from the time when Israel came out of Egypt (the exodus) and headed for the land given to them by God. As Israel came into Moab, the Moabites sent for a man named Balaam, who was a prophet and spiritual man. They asked him to come and curse Israel and prevent Israel from being able take control of Moab. The elders of Moab understood the need to win a battle in the spirit realm, and they felt that Balaam was the best man to do this. From the very first time, Balaam sought God about going and cursing Jacob. God said, "No, they are blessed. Don't go." Ultimately, Balaam went anyway and attempted to curse Jacob (Israel), but each time, his words actually would bless Jacob. Balaam attempted several times from several locations, but the results were always the same—only blessings. At the end of Numbers 24, Balaam turned from simply blessing Jacob to prophesying about events that would happen between Israel, Moab, and Edom in the latter days.

> And now, behold, I go to my people: come therefore, and I will advertise thee what this people shall do to thy people <u>in the latter days</u>.
>
> (17) I shall see him, but not now: I shall behold him, but not nigh: there shall come a star out of Jacob, and a <u>Sceptre</u> shall rise out of Israel, and shall smite the corners of Moab, and destroy all the children of Sheth. (18) And Edom shall be a possession,.... (19) Out of Jacob shall come <u>he that shall have dominion</u>, and shall destroy him that remaineth of the city. (Numbers 24:14, 17–19)

This prophecy is for a time that is not near (nigh) but is in the latter times. When the star of Jacob, the king. comes, he has a Sceptre and he has dominion over the nations and the city. This king of Israel, whose title is the Sceptre, is none other than the Messiah. He shall destroy parts of Moab and control Edom. Both of these locations are in the southern part of modern-day Jordan. The city referred to is Jerusalem. He will destroy his enemies who remain in the city.

It is important to note that when the vile king comes into Israel, as seen in Daniel 11, both Edom and Moab escape his control.

> He [the vile king] shall enter also into the glorious land, and many countries shall be overthrown: but these shall escape out of his hand, even <u>Edom</u>, and <u>Moab</u>, and the chief of the children of Ammon.

The Messiah overthrows Edom and Moab, not the vile king. The vile king controls most, if not all, of the other surrounding nations, but these two escape, only to be destroyed by the Messiah when he comes to set up his kingdom and dominion. The direct intervention by the Messiah is the result of the elders of Moab trying to curse Israel when they came in from Egypt.

This Messianic battle against Edom and Moab also is seen in Isaiah 63.

> (1)Who is this that cometh from <u>Edom</u>, with dyed garments from Bozrah? This that is glorious in his apparel, travelling in the greatness of his strength? I speak in righteousness mighty to save. (2) Wherefore art thou red in thine apparel, and thy garments like him that treadeth in the winefat? (3) <u>I have trodden the winepress</u> alone; and of the people there was none with me: for I will tread them [Edom] in mine anger, and trample them in my fury; and their blood shall be sprinkled upon my garments, and <u>I will stain all my raiment</u>. (4) For the <u>day of vengeance</u> is in my heart, and the <u>year of my redeemed is come</u>.

This treading of the winepress also is seen in Revelation 19:

> And I [John] saw heaven opened, and behold a white horse; and he that sat upon him was called Faithful and True, and in righteousness he doth judge and make war. (12) His eyes were

as a flame of fire, and on his head were many crowns; and he had a name written, that no man knew, but he himself. (13) And he was clothed with a <u>vesture dipped in blood</u>: and his name is called the Word of God.(14) And the armies which were in heaven followed him upon white horses, clothed in fine linen, white and clean (15) And out of his mouth goeth a sharp sword, that with it he should smite the nations: and he shall rule [dominion] them with a rod of iron: and <u>he treadeth the winepress</u> of the fierceness and wrath of Almighty God. (Revelation 19:11–15)

It is clear that the prophecy of Balaam, given to him by God, is to be fulfilled in the days of the end, at a time when the Messiah judges the nations. With this time frame established, we can assess the remaining portion of the prophecy.

(21) And he [Balaam] looked on the Kenites, and took up his parable, and said, strong is thy dwelling place, and thou puttest thy nest in a rock. (22)Nevertheless the Kenite shall be wasted, until <u>Asshur</u> shall carry thee away captive. (23) And he took up his parable, and said, Alas, who shall live [survive] when God doeth this! (24) And <u>ships shall come from the coast</u> of Chittim, and shall <u>afflict Asshur</u>.

Asshur wastes the Kenites (an area of Jordan). They do not escape from him; they are led away captive. We are asked who can survive this amazing time of God's vengeance; it echoes the statement from Matthew 24:22

except those days should be shortened, there should no flesh be saved.

We see that the ships of Chittim shall afflict Asshur. Asshur is the name of Assyria or Assyrians. How can the Assyrians attack and control much of the Middle East at the same time as the vile king from Persia? What we have is a tie between the Persian king and Asshur the Assyrian. The ships of Chittim don't come against two kings at the same time in the same location; they come against a Persian king called Asshur. The fourth king to rise from Persia is not honored with the kingdom, but he gets his power from a small people. I've already mentioned that he would come from one of the many minority peoples in Iran (modern Persia). Asshur is one of the minority peoples in Iran, part of the old nation of Assyria, located in northern Iran in the Lake Ermia area. In the current Islamic republic of Iran, the Assyrians have been given a seat in the government at the parliamentary level. They hold one of five seats granted to minorities. Thus, the Assyrians have their own representative in the Iranian parliament, although he cannot move beyond this status in leadership because he is a Christian. Assyrians in Iran are a minority not only ethnically but also as a religious group— Christian. It is inconceivable that the Assyrians of Iran would elect a non-Christian as their representative, as nearly all Assyrians (more than 94 percent) in Iran are Christian. Their current Assyrian leader is indeed Christian.

The vile king will be <u>Persian by nationality</u> and citizenship but will be <u>ethnically Assyrian</u> and <u>Christian by religion</u>. However, <u>just because he claims to be Christian, does not make him devout or sanctified</u>. If he were either, he would not be vile. When he is under pressure, he will turn against the holy covenant and attack the people of the covenant, Israel.

We see a battle in Micah 5 between the Messiah and an Assyrian in the land of Israel and Jerusalem. The account reinforces the Assyrian, Messiah, and Israel connection seen in Numbers 24. It will happen in the last days, at the time of the Messianic intervention. The Messiah will come from Bethlehem and become ruler in Israel. He will deliver Israel from the Assyrian.

> Now gather thyself in troops, O daughter of troops: he [the Assyrian] hath laid siege against us [Israel]; they shall smite the judge of Israel with a rod upon the cheek. (2) but thou, <u>Bethlehem</u> Ephratah, though thou be little among the thousands of Judah, yet out of thee shall he come forth unto me that is <u>to be ruler in Israel</u>; whose goings forth have been <u>from old, from everlasting</u>. [the Messiah]. (3) Therefore will he give them up,

until the time that she which travaileth hath brought forth:
then the remnant of his brethren shall return unto the children
of Israel (4) And he shall stand and feed in the strength of the
LORD, in the majesty of the name of the Lord his God; and
they shall abide: for now shall he be great unto the ends of
the earth. (5) And this man [the Messiah] shall be the peace,
when the Assyrian [Asshur] shall come into our land [Israel]:
and when he shall tread in our palaces [Jerusalem], then shall
we raise against him seven shepherds and eight principle men.
(6) And they shall waste the land of Assyria with the sword,
and the land of Nimrod in the entrances thereof: thus shall he
[the Messiah] deliver us from the Assyrian [Asshur], when he
[Asshur, the man] cometh into our land [Israel], and when he
treadeth within our borders. (Micah 5:1–6)

We see in Daniel 11:31 that the king will take away the daily
sacrifice and place the abomination that maketh desolate. This same
act is done by the little horn in Daniel 8:11. The little horn comes up
from within one of Alexander's general's empires—from one of the
four horns. From Daniel 11, we see that the Persian king is the little
horn, and the king is called the Assyrian. The Assyrian is the little horn
that comes up in the midst of the ten horns, and the empire is the old
Seleucid empire, located in the modern-day Iranian area.

It needs to be noted that under the control and leadership of Asshur,
the land of Assyria will be reunited and restored. This means that at
some point in the future, the Iraqi area of old Assyria will join with the
Iranian portion. This is seen in Isaiah 23.

Behold the land of the Chaldeans [Assyria]; this people [nation]
was not, till the Assyrian founded it for them that dwell in
the wilderness [Diaspora]: they set up the towers thereof, they
raised up the palaces thereof; and he brought it to ruin. (Isaiah
23:13)

The reference to the ruin of Assyria is the battle seen in Micah 5:6,
when the Israelis, under the leadership of the Messiah, wastes Assyria.
We resume our study of Daniel 11.

And such as do wickedly against the covenant shall he [the Assyrian] corrupt by flatteries: but the people that do know their God shall be strong, and do exploits. (33) And they that understand among the people shall instruct many, yet they shall fall by the sword, and by the flame, by captivity, and by spoil, many days: (34) Now when they shall fall, they shall be holpen with little help: but many shall cleave to them with flatteries. (35) And some of them of understanding shall fall, to try them, and to purge, and to make them white, even to the time of the end: because it is yet for a time appointed. (11:32–35)

These Scriptures show how desperate these times will be and how great the disparity will be between the people of God and the people of the Assyrian. On one hand, there is wickedness and corruption; on the other, strength and exploits. Yet while some will know God and understand and instruct many, they still will be killed for their support of God. There will be almost no help for them from others; they will stand nearly alone, and those who say they support them, but don't, will be exposed as flatterers. We are told that all of the afflictions of these righteous people are for a reason—to try them, to make them white, and to purge them. They will become worthy of participating in God's army when he comes to defeat the Assyrian and his armies. This is seen in Revelation 19:14.

And the armies which were in heaven followed him upon horses, clothed in fine linen, <u>white and clean</u>.

Daniel 11 continues:

(36) And the king shall do according to his will, and shall exalt himself, and magnify himself above every god, and shall speak marvelous things against the God of gods, and shall prosper till the indignation be accomplished: for that that is determined shall be done.(37) Neither shall he regard the God of his fathers, nor the desire of women, nor regard any god: for he shall magnify himself above all. (38) But in his estate shall he honour the God of forces; and a god whom his fathers knew

not shall he honour with gold, and silver, and with precious stones, and pleasant things. (39) Thus shall he do in the most strong holds with a strange god, whom he shall acknowledge and increase with glory; and he shall cause them to rule over many, and shall divide the land for gain.

These Scriptures give us a very detailed understanding of the Assyrian and allow us to see what motivates him and what he values. We are told that he does not regard the God of his fathers. It means he does not regard his Christian upbringing or the God of the Bible. Yet we know he must pretend to have faith in order to represent a nation of Christians. This man is so arrogant that he does not regard any god. He exalts himself above all gods, even the God of his fathers. It does not mean that he does not believe in the gods; it simply means he sees himself as above them. We are told that he even honours them with money and things of value, but he will not worship them. He is not above using them to attain his goals of world conquest, vengeance, and the worship of men. I don't believe the reference to the desire of woman means that he won't be married or have children but rather, he simply does not feel a need for any of those relationships. He will have a wife and family if he feels it will promote his agenda. He will get very close to strange gods because it promotes his agenda. He always does his will; he will not submit to anyone.

In Daniel 11:40—45, we see a series of military campaigns involving this king and many nations they include Egypt, the king of the south; Russia, the king of the north; Libya, Ethiopia, the kings of the east, China; Japan, India and the Middle East. It would require an entire chapter to do justice to these six verses, but it is not directly relevant to this study so we will stop here.

Summary of Daniel 11

1. Four kings will come up from Persia, The fourth king will cause the daily sacrifice to cease and will set up the abomination of desolation in the temple. He is the same king as the little horn, seen in Daniel 8. He will be the leader of ten horns.

2. He will rise to power through a small people, a minority.

3. He will be a vile man, a liar, as well as a flatterer who will pretend to be a man of peace. He ultimately will use armies to get his way.

4. He will attack and defeat Egypt in the last days.

5. He will believe himself to be god and will also use other gods to attain his agenda.

6. He is a Persian by nationality and citizenship; ethnically and religiously he is an Assyrian.

7. He will turn against the holy covenant and will persecute God's people, the people of the covenant.

CHAPTER FIVE

Revelation 17

Why study the book of Revelation as part of a study of Daniel? Actually, if the book of Revelation covers and explains events at the end of the age, it is reasonable to expect that we would find references to those same events and characters in Daniel. I believe that's exactly what happens—the events can be coordinated and the same characters can be identified. The terms and descriptions are not word for word, but they certainly are identifiable. The big reason for harmonizing the two books is that we get many confirmations and some clarifications, which paint a more accurate picture and understanding of the events.

While the title of this chapter is "Revelation 17," we first will draw some information from chapters 12 and 13 to set the stage for chapter 17. We also will look at parts of chapters 18 and 19 as continuations of chapter 17. Unlike most of the Daniel scriptural studies, where I provided the text of virtually all the Scriptures within the chapter, for Revelation 17, I will pull out individual or groups of Scriptures, expounding on and comparing them. (Readers will need to study the full text to satisfy any questions or concerns they may have.)

The primary topics to be covered in Revelations are the progression of empires, the ten-horned empire, and the little horn, as well as Daniel's people, all found in the book of Daniel.

<u>Revelation 12</u>

(12:1) And there appeared a great wonder [a sign] in heaven; a woman clothed with the sun, and the moon under her feet, and upon her head a crown of twelve stars: (2) And she being with child cried, travailing in birth, and pained to be delivered. (3) And there appeared another wonder in heaven; and behold a great red dragon, having seven heads and ten horns, and seven crowns upon his heads. (4) And his tail drew the third part of the stars of heaven, and cast them to the earth: and the dragon stood before the woman which was ready to be delivered, for to devour her child as soon as it was born. (5) And she brought forth a man-child, who was to rule all nations with a rod of iron: and her child was caught up unto God, and to his throne. (6) And the woman fled into the wilderness, where she hath a place prepared of God, that they should feed her there a thousand two hundred threescore days.

We see two great signs in heaven—not the actual events but symbols and sequences representing the events. The first sign is the woman clothed with the sun, and the moon under her feet, and upon her head a crown of twelve stars.

This woman represents the nation or family of Israel. We know this because the same symbols were used to represent Jacob and his family in the dream given to Jacob's son Joseph in the book of Genesis:

And he [Joseph] dreamed yet another dream, and told his brethren, and said, Behold, I have dreamed a dream more; and behold, the <u>sun and the moon and the eleven stars</u> made obeisance to me. (10) And he told it to his father, and to his brethren, and his father rebuked him, and said unto him, What is this dream that thou hast dreamed? Shall I [Jacob] and thy mother and thy brethren indeed come to bow down ourselves to thee to the earth? (37:9–10)

Joseph himself would be the twelfth star, and the crown on the woman's head represents the twelve tribes of Israel. This woman, Israel, would bring forth the man-child who is destined to rule the world with a rod of iron. He is caught up to God to heaven, to his throne. This is the Messiah. The term "caught up" is the Greek word, *harpazo*, which means to be taken by force. For Christians, this event is seen in the book of Acts:

> To whom also he [Jesus] shewed himself alive after his passion by many infallible proofs, being seen of them <u>forty days</u>, and speaking of the things pertaining to the kingdom of God: ....(9) And when he had spoken these things, while they [his disciples] beheld, <u>he was taken up</u>; and a cloud received him out of their sight. (10) And while they looked stedfastly toward heaven as he went up, behold, two men stood by them in white apparel; (11) Which also said, Ye men of Galilee, why stand ye gazing up into heaven? This same Jesus, which is <u>taken from you into heaven</u>, shall so come in like manner as ye have seen him go into heaven. (Acts 1:3, 9–11)

The dragon, as seen in Revelation 12:4, attempts to destroy the child as soon as he is born. This also is seen by Christians as the account of Herod's killing of the children in and around Bethlehem. He had been told that the Messiah would come from Bethlehem (Matthew 2:1–7).

God prepares a place for the woman, Israel, in the wilderness where she can flee—a place where she can survive for a period of three and one-half years—1,260 days. This corresponds to Daniel's time, times, and a dividing of time, when Jerusalem is trodden under foot. This is the time of Daniel's little horn, the Persian king, the Assyrian.

The second sign is the great red dragon. Again, we see symbolic representations of persons and events, not the actual persons or events. The dragon drew a third part of the angels of heaven and caused them to fall, he is personally responsible for this tragedy. We see that the dragon has seven heads and ten horns, and that the heads have crowns on them. The crowns indicate that the heads are kingdoms or empires. The ten horns represent individual kings or leaders. These interpretations will be shown more clearly later in this chapter.

Revelation 12 continues:

(7) And there was war in heaven: Michael and his angels fought against the dragon; and the dragon fought and his angels,(8) and prevailed not; neither was their place found any more in heaven.(9) And the great dragon was cast out, that old serpent, called the Devil, and Satan, which deceiveth the whole world: he was cast out into the earth, and his angels were cast out with him...(12) Therefore rejoice, ye heavens, and ye that dwell in them. Woe to the inhabiters of the earth and of the sea! For the devil is come down to you, having great wrath, because he knoweth that he hath but a short time.

This war is a spiritual war fought in the heavens, and the dragon and his angels did not prevail. They were cast down into the earth. This battle is not a battle that was fought and won in ancient times; rather, it is a battle that is being fought and is nearing its end right now. We are living in the time just before the manifestation of the ten horns and the Assyrian. We know the time is short, and so does the dragon. The activity of the dark spiritual powers, in the affairs of men will be ever increasing, Woe to the inhabitants of the earth.

(13) And when the dragon saw that he was cast unto the earth, <u>he persecuted the woman</u> which brought forth the man child. (14) And to the woman were given two wings of a great eagle, that she might fly into the wilderness, into <u>her place</u>, where she is nourished for <u>a time, and times, and a half a time</u>, from the face of the serpent.

Here we see how strong Satan's hatred is for the Jewish people and the Jewish Messiah she brought forth. She must flee from him to the place that God prepared for her as a refuge. This refuge is in the wilderness of Edom, because as shown earlier, it is the only location that escapes the Assyrian's control. Also the battle by the Messiah to liberate Jerusalem starts in Edom, where he delivers his people;

Who is this that cometh from Edom,...I have trodden the winepress... and I will stain all my raiment, and the year of my redeemed is come. (Isaiah 63:1–4)

The second sign in heaven, the red dragon—seven heads and ten horns—clearly represents <u>Satan's kingdom</u> and shows that it is diametrically opposed to God and his people. The symbols shown in this second sign represent the pattern and components of Satan's kingdom.

<u>Revelation 13</u>

(1) And I [John] stood upon the sand of the sea, and I saw a beast rise up out of the sea, having seven heads and ten horns, and upon his horns ten crowns, and upon his heads <u>the name</u> of blasphemy.(2) And the beast which I saw was like unto a <u>leopard</u>, and his feet were as the feet of a <u>bear</u>, and his mouth as the mouth of a <u>lion</u>: and the dragon gave him his power, and his seat, and great authority.

John sees a beast rise up from the sea, just as Daniel did. This beast has the same components and pattern as Satan's kingdom, as seen in Revelation 12. We are told that the beast receives its power and authority from the dragon, Satan. The direction and goals of this beast come from Satan. This beast is expediting Satan's will and desires. We now see that the ten horns are, in fact, ten kings because they wear crowns, and the heads now wear "<u>the name</u> of blasphemy"—the name of their leader, Satan. Satan originated blasphemy, which is to slander and rail against God, when he drew the third part of the angels from heaven.

The beast seen by John has the same components as Daniel's beast, except the lion, bear, and leopard are incorporated into <u>a single beast</u>, and seen as <u>one beast</u> with ten horns. The lion, bear, and leopard are integral operational parts of the beast. They don't just lose their dominion, as seen in Daniel, but now are used as assets within the beast's kingdom.

I believe this beast represents the feet and ten toes of Nebuchadnezzar's great image. This also would mean that the vision of Daniel 7 was not just four independent empires rising up and then falling but actually was the sequential process or development of the two feet and ten toes. They represent the end-time rising of the final beast upon which the final judgment of God will fall.

If this is true, and lion-hearted England with its empire represents the lion, then the feet and toes began to be manifest in 1920, when

England controlled Palestine. It has continued through to the Russian bear and now into the development of the current militant Islamic caliphate, which the leopard represents. The leopard is fated to be replaced by the ten-horned military alliance, which eventually will control the same area as the old Roman Empire.

Revelation 13 continues:

> (3) And I saw one of his heads as it were wounded to death; and his deadly wound was healed: and all the world wondered after the beast. (4) And they worshipped the dragon, which gave power unto the beast: and they worshipped the beast, saying, Who is like unto the beast? Who is able to make war with him?

Here, we see that the beast is the strongest military entity on earth. They ask, who can make war with him? We also see clearly that at the top of the beast is a man—"him"—and yet the wound to the head is not to him personally but to one of the heads. I believe that as we study farther in Revelation that we can identify which head is wounded.

> (5) And there was given unto him a mouth speaking great things and blasphemies; and power was given unto him to continue forty and two months. (6) And he opened his mouth in blasphemy against God, to blaspheme his name, and his tabernacle, and them that dwell in heaven. (7) And it was given unto him to make war with the saints, and to overcome them: and power was given him over <u>all kindreds, and tongues, and nations</u>. (8) And all that dwell upon the earth shall worship him, whose names are not written in the book of life of the Lamb slain from the foundation of the world. (9) If any man have an ear, let him hear. (10) He that leadeth into captivity shall go into captivity: he that killeth with the sword must be killed with the sword. Here is the patience and the faith of the saints.

We see the arrogance and anger that the beast has—a reflection of Satan's anger—and that he belittles God, and all that pertains to God.

Everything that God values, he blasphemes—God's name, his temple, and God's people who live in heaven. The beast, the vile Persian, the little horn, and the Assyrian all are names for the <u>same man</u>. He is given power to continue for forty-two months, which is three and one-half years, or 1,260 days, or time, times, and half of time. No matter how it is said, it is the same time and the same man, committing the same atrocities against Jerusalem, God, and his people.

We also can see that the scope of his control is not limited to Persia and the Middle East but extends to the whole earth and every nation and tongue. No matter your family connections language, or ethnic background, you will be subject to him. Only those whose names are written in God's book of life will refuse to worship and submit to him. The people of the world at large actually will bow down and worship this man. They will believe that he and the dragon are deities and worthy to be worshipped. What an incredibly sad time this will be. Is it any wonder that this is the time when God will judge the nations?

In Revelation 13:9–10, God sends a message to his people concerning this point in time. He says, "If any man hath an ear, let him hear." If you have a desire to hear what God is saying, then listen: "He [the Assyrian] **that leadeth** [the world] **into captivity** [as prisoners] **shall also be taken captive** [taken prisoner by God]**: also he (the Assyrian) that has been killing people all over the world must also be killed in the end." It will require faith and patience by God's people to persevere this happens. He will not go unpunished.**

In verses 11–18, we are introduced to a second beast that is an important accomplice for the Assyrian and is actually the person who accomplishes many of the administrative tasks needed to subdue and control the world and its people. The accomplice (false prophet) is not the focus of this study but does require some explanation because of the role he plays. He is a religious man who appears to be a lamb, but when he speaks, he is anything but a lamb; he speaks as a dragon. Those who have spiritual discernment will be able to tell that he is not from God. Most of the world is deceived, however, and will follow him and the Assyrian. This man will do great signs and wonders; he is known as the false prophet from Revelation 19:20. He will be thrown into the lake that burneth with fire, along with the beast.

(11) And I beheld another beast coming up out of the earth; and he had <u>two horns like a lamb</u>, and he <u>spake as a dragon.</u> (12) And he exerciseth all the power of the first beast before him, and causeth the earth and them which dwell therein to <u>worship the first beast</u>, whose deadly wound was healed. (13) And he <u>doeth great wonders</u>, so that he maketh fire come down from heaven on the earth in the sight of men, (14) And deceiveth them that dwell on the earth by the means of those miracles which he had power to do in the sight of the beast; saying to them that dwell on the earth, that they should make an image to the beast, which had the wound by a sword, and did live. (15) And he had power to give life unto the image of the beast, that the image of the beast should both speak, and cause that <u>as many as would not worship the image of the beast should be killed</u>. (16) And he causeth all, both small great, rich and poor , free and bond, to receive a mark in their right hand, or their foreheads: (17) And <u>that no man might buy or sell</u>, save he that had the mark, or the name of the beast, or the number of his name. (18) Here is wisdom, Let him that hath understanding count the number of the beast; for it is the number of a man; and <u>his number is six hundred threescore and six.</u>

The image of the beast will do two things: it will speak, and it will be a killing machine—the image will cause people to be killed.

The final task ascribed to this false prophet is the mark of the beast. He causes everyone—small and great, rich and poor, free and bonded—to receive a mark in the right hand or on the forehead. This mark identifies the people as belonging to the Assyrian's kingdom, and except you have the mark you cannot buy or sell. The Assyrian will control the world's economy completely, and without fidelity to him and his government, no one will be able to operate within it. Some will receive just a mark, some the name of the Assyrian, and others the number of his name. We are not left to speculate about the number itself—it is "chi xi stigma," the numeric value of six hundred and sixty six. The number represents the Assyrian's name. This sexagesimal number is an Assyrian number, as the Assyrian numbering system is a base sixty system, rather than the base ten system we usually use today.

The only king known in history to have had a number for his name is the Assyrian Sargon II. (His number was 16,280, but the number itself is not relevant to this study.) The king's name, "Sargon," comes from the Bible, but in Assyrian records, his name was Sharrukin, which means "the legitimate king." The fact that the end-time Assyrian king also would have a number for his name should not surprise us. Historians tell us that Sargon II took his name from Sargon the Great, an earlier king, to legitimize his authority and reign. It would also seem likely that the new Assyrian/Persian king would desire to connect himself to previous Assyrian dynasties.

It is interesting that the current modern Assyrian nationalist movement, which is spearheaded by the Assyrian Universal Alliance (AUA), uses the insignia of Sargon as a finial atop their new national Assyrian flag (See photo on page 74). It seems that they desire to tie their new nation to its pre-Christian roots—a point that's also made by their new flag prominently displaying their old pagan deity, Asshur (See photos on pages 75 & 76). It is likely that any contemporary revived Assyrian homeland will come through the efforts of the AUA and other associated organizations, Their views and leadership will be important to their success.

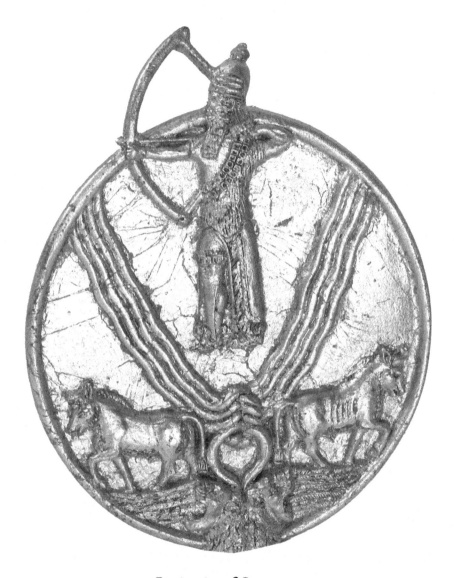

Insignia of Sargon

as used on the new Assyrian flag

New Assyrian Flag

Note the Assyrian star at the center

The symbol of the Assyrian god Asshur

Revelation 17

The main focus of Revelation 17 is the judgment of a woman called the great whore. This great whore is of interest to us because she can be tied to Daniel's visions and the final empire of ten horns.

> (1) And there came one of the seven angels which had the seven vials, and talked with me, Come hither; I will shew unto thee the judgment of the great whore that sitteth upon many waters: (2) With whom the kings of the earth have committed fornication, and the inhabitants of the earth have been made drunk with the wine of her fornication. (3) So he carried me away in the spirit into the wilderness: and I saw a woman sit upon a scarlet coloured beast, full of the names of blasphemy, having seven heads and ten horns. (4) And the woman was arrayed in purple and scarlet colour, and decked with gold and precious stones and pearls, having a golden cup in her hand full of abominations and the filthiness of her fornication: (5) And upon her forehead was a name written, Mystery, Babylon the Great, the Mother of Harlots and Abominations of the Earth. (6) And I saw the woman drunken with the blood of the saints, and with the blood of the martyrs of Jesus: and when I saw her, I wondered with great admiration.

This is a spiritual vision, because John was carried away in the spirit, and his host was an angel. The angel's intent is to shew John the judgment of Babylon the Great. The term "shew" is the Greek word *dieknuo*, which means "to expose to the eyes." As John looks at the woman, he sees her sitting on a scarlet colored beast having seven heads and ten horns. We know this beast from Revelation 12 and 13. The beast is the kingdom of Satan, the red dragon. The woman is not Satan's kingdom but is seen riding atop the beast, so there is a relationship. We also know that she is not godly but rather is full of the blood of the saints. She is also seen as very wealthy and prosperous. The identity of this woman has been a mystery. She is the mother of harlots and abominations of the earth. Babylon can be traced all the way back to Nimrod and Babel, the very first kingdom after the great flood of

Noah. All false religions and doctrines have come through Babylon via the progression of civilization to us today. This woman is carrying the spirit of Babylon.

The nation of Babylon ended about 130 BC (the last king of Babylon) and had been in ruins for two hundred years at the time that John received his vision. There will be a new revived nation of Babylon, to be found in the last days. She will be called "the daughter of Babylon." This daughter of Babylon will be discussed in more detail later in this book.

The great whore is seen sitting upon many waters—this is in reference to many peoples, many ethnic groups. We see this clarified in verse 15.

> The waters which thou sawest, where the whore sitteth, are peoples, and multitudes, and nations, and tongues. (Rev. 17:15)

The vision of Revelation 17 continues:

> (7) And the angel said to me, Wherefore didst thou marvel? I will tell thee the mystery of the woman, and the beast that carrieth her, which hath the seven heads and ten horns.(8) The beast that thou sawest was, and is not; and shall ascend out of the bottomless pit, and go into perdition: and they that dwell on the earth shall wonder, whose names were not written in the book of life from the foundation of the world, when they behold the beast that was, and is not, and yet is.

Johns' reaction to the woman seems to have surprised or perplexed the angel, the angel asks John, why did you marvel?" This is a legitimate question. It's hard to understand why John marvels when he sees the abominations and the blood of the saints. John does not respond, but it seems that John is marveling at the opulence and appearance of the woman, not the antichrist spirit. Based on the time in which she exists, which is at the end of the age, she represents the pinnacle of man's achievements and technology. All of the amazing technology and accomplishments of man, however, will not negate the price that men will pay for sin and rebellion when God judges men's hearts.

The angel tells John, "I will <u>tell thee</u> the mystery of the woman and of the beast that carrieth her." The angel has, at least for the moment, changed the focus from showing the judgment of the woman to telling John the mystery of the woman and beast. The term "tell" is the Greek word "ereo" which means "to speak an utterance."

We are told that this beast "was" and "is not" and "yet is." This is a sequence. The beast started and continued until a point in time when it stopped—"is not"—and then at some point, it starts again. It comes out of the pit—"yet is"—and continues until it ends and enters perdition (hell). The people who make up the empire, who are not in God's book, are destined for hell.

This is the same sequence we find from Daniel 2 and Daniel 7, where we see the empires come through time until they reach the end of the two legs of iron, which is the end of the Roman Empire in 1458 (the fall of Constantinople to the Ottoman Empire). The two feet and the ten toes did not immediately follow the Romans. The Islamic caliphate of the Ottomans prevented the establishment of an independent Egypt, Jordan, Syria, and Israel. The Ottomans ruled the eastern Roman Empire for nearly five hundred years; this is the "is not" time of the beast. But the Ottomans are defeated in the First World War. England, the British lion, came to power in 1920, and the sequence resumed—the "yet is" time has come. We now are watching as the nations are established and the proper alignments are made.

The explanation in Revelation 17 continues:

> (9) And here is the mind that hath wisdom. The seven heads are seven mountains, on which the woman sitteth. (10) And there are seven kings: five are fallen, and one is, and the other is not yet come; and when he cometh, he must continue a short space.

The seven heads are seven mountains. These are not literally mountains but things that have risen or have yet to rise. The Greek word is "oros" , which means "to lift up." I've come to the conclusion that the mountains are more akin to foundations upon which the woman sits. We are told they are seven kings (or kingdoms) and that five have fallen, one "is," and one is yet to come. If the one that "is" refers to the

Roman Empire—the existing empire at the time of John's vision—then the five fallen empires would progress backwards from the Romans. The five empires would be Assyrian, Babylonian, Median, Persian, and Grecian. The head that is yet to come will be the Assyrian, including the ten horns, lion, bear, and leopard (see charts on pages 86 & 87).

(11) And the beast that was, and is not, even he is the eighth, and is of the seven, and goeth into perdition. (12) And the ten horns which thou sawest are ten kings, which have received no kingdom as yet; but receive power as kings one hour with the beast. (13) These have one mind, and shall give their power and strength unto the beast.

The man who represents the final beast, whose roots extend back to ancient times, is considered to be the eighth and last head. He comes from the seven and is of the seven, but he is separate, in that he comes up last. It should be noted here that the head that receives a deadly wound is one of the seven (Revelation 13:3), not the eighth.

I believe that the wound to the head of one of the seven heads refers to one of the old heads from which the eighth king comes. He is a Persian by nationality but ethnically an Assyrian. He is referred to in Scripture a multitude of times as "the Assyrian." When the Assyrian is killed, an army of Israelis, under the leadership of the Messiah from Bethlehem, will go to Assyria, attack it, and waste it. This military campaign seems far-fetched, as there currently is no nation of Assyria. The final parting blows of the Ottoman Empire was an attempt to eradicate the entire Assyrian people and to end any hope of a future Assyrian nation. This wound to the head of one of the seven is severe, but God says there will be a revived Assyria, and the Assyrian will be the man that establishes it for the Assyrian peoples that are in Diaspora around the world.

Behold the land of the Chaldeans [Assyrians]; this people [nation] was not, till the Assyrian founded it for them that dwell in the wilderness. (Isaiah 23:13)

Today the terms Chaldeans and Assyrians are used interchangeably; they are the same people. Watch for the sign of Assyria's revival.

We see the ten horns, just as we did in Daniel 7, and we are told they are kings, just like in Daniel 7. However, in this account we find some additional information—these kings don't have kingdoms, but they have authority or power as kings. These are pseudo-kings. They don't rule over a kingdom or have a nation to control; they don't have to deal with economic or social issues. These kings deal only with the power of the kingdom and the military strength and its projection and use. They have one mind; they are in consensus, and give their power and strength to the beast. The strength represents the military assets they have under their authority and control. The Greek word used for king is "basileus", which can be used for more meanings than just king; it also can mean, prince, leader, or commander. I believe that the term "commander" best defines who these men are. They are ten military commanders who control all the military might of a military alliance rising out of the area of both the eastern and western old Roman Empires. This military alliance is short-lived—it will only operate for one hour with the beast.

As mentioned in chapter three of this book, the current military alliance of NATO nearly matches the requirements seen above.

The vision in Revelation 17 continues:

> (14) These [kings] shall make war with the Lamb, and the Lamb shall overcome them: for he is Lord of lords, and King of kings: and they that are with him are called, and chosen, and faithful. (15) And he saith unto me, The waters which thou sawest, where the whore sitteth, are peoples, and multitudes, and nations, and tongues. (16) And the ten horns which thou sawest upon the beast, these shall hate the whore, and shall make her desolate and naked, and shall eat her flesh, and burn her with fire. (17) For God hath put in their hearts to fulfill his will, and to agree, and give their kingdom unto the beast, until the words of God shall be fulfilled.(18) And the woman which thou sawest is that great city, which <u>reigneth over the kings</u> of the earth.

While there is a relationship between the ten horns and the great whore, Babylon the Great, it appears that they hate her enough to destroy her and burn her with fire. They have given their authority and power unto the beast, and under his leadership they remove her from riding over them. It should be noted that these kings believe that they are fighting God and doing everything they can to defeat God; they, in fact, are doing his will by giving away their authority to the beast. I'm sure that if they'd known this was in God's plan, they would not do it. These ten commanders don't limit their hatred to just Babylon. Shortly after they destroy Babylon, they turn their focus on fighting the Messiah when he comes. We are told that they are overcome, defeated by the Messiah because he is the Lord of lords and King of kings. The Messiah is not alone when he returns, and they that are with him are called faithful and chosen. This is God's army. These events also are seen in Revelation 19:11–21.

> (11) And I saw heaven opened, and behold a white horse; and he that sat upon him was called faithful and true, and in righteousness he doth judge and make war. (12) His eyes were as a flame of fire, and on his head were many crowns; and he had a name written, that no man knew, but he himself. (13) And he was clothed with a vesture dipped in blood [he comes from Edom, Isa.63]: and his name is called the Word of God. (14) And the armies which were in heaven followed him upon white horses, clothed in fine linen, white and clean. (15) And out of his mouth goeth a sharp sword, that with it he should smite the nations: and he shall rule them with a rod of iron [the man-child from the woman, Rev.12]: and he treadeth the winepress [Isa.63] of the fierceness and wrath of almighty God. (16) And he hath on his vesture and on his thigh a name written, KING OF KINGS, AND LORD OF LORDS [Rev. 17]. (17) And I saw an angel standing in the sun; and he cried with a load voice, saying to all the fowls that fly in the midst of heaven, Come and gather yourselves together unto the supper of the great God. (18) That ye may eat the flesh of kings, and the flesh of captains, and the flesh of mighty men, and the flesh of horses, and of them that sit on them, and the flesh of all men, both free and bond, both small and great. (19) And I saw the beast, and the kings of the earth, and their armies, gathered together to make war against him that sat on the horse, and

against his army. (20) And the beast was taken, and with him the false prophet that wrought miracles before him, with which he deceived them that had received the mark of the beast, and them that worshipped his image. These both were cast alive into the lake of fire burning with brimstone. (21) And the remnant were slain with the sword of him that sat upon the horse, which sword proceeded out of his mouth: and all the fowls were filled with their flesh.

We read in Revelation 17 that the King of kings shall overcome them—what an understatement! Here we see that the world's armies and everyone associated with them will pay the price for their rebellion. You certainly don't want to be on the wrong side of this battle.

The last statement in Revelation 17:18 says that the great city that was seen is that great city that reigns over the kings of the earth. This statement, given about the woman, is the only statement made about her, after the angel says he will tell John about her and the beast. Most of the descriptions and definitions are given about the beast only, not the woman. Nowhere in chapter seventeen do we find the angel showing the judgment of the woman. This statement is seen in two different ways. The first is that the city is that city that reigns over the kings in John's day, at the time of the writing of the book. This would lead us to believe that Babylon the Great is the Roman Empire and its capital city, Rome. This view is difficult for me to understand, unlike some other scriptural sequences where we can see that the reference is made back to the Roman Empire, such as early in Revelation 17, where it is stated that five heads are fallen, one is, and one has not yet come. I find no such sequence or indicator in Rev. 17:18. The second view of Rev. 17:18 is that it is meant to apply to the time of the fulfillment of the vision. This would mean that the woman reigns over the kings of the earth at the time of the end. This would explain why the ten kings hate her and throw off her control. Also, the beast can't control the world as long as Babylon is riding atop both him and his military alliance. This second view does not fit with modern Rome as Babylon. While Rome—Vatican City—has a lot of influence over the millions of the world's Catholics and as such, plays a part in the policy-making of the predominantly Catholic nations, modern Rome does not reign over the kings of the earth and certainly does not exercise control over the leadership of NATO—the ten horns.

The angel of Revelation 17:1 stated that he would "shew the judgment of the great whore," Babylon the great. This does not happen in Revelation 17. In Revelation 18, we find that the subject does not change, except that <u>Babylon the Great is judged</u>. The following list of Scriptures will demonstrate her judgment:

> And he [another angel] cried mightily with a strong voice, saying, <u>Babylon the Great is fallen</u>, is fallen, and is <u>become</u> the habitation of devils, and the hold of every foul spirit, and the cage of every unclean and hateful bird. (3) For all nations have drunk of the wine of the wrath of her fornication, and the kings of the earth have committed fornication with her, and the merchants of the earth are waxed rich through the abundance of her delicacies. (Revelation 18:2–3)

Clearly, this is the same Babylon the Great as is seen in Revelation 17. We are told she is fallen because she has <u>become</u> the habitation of devils and hold of every foul spirit. Babylon was not always full of demons but became that way. This is a change—she was once something different; a golden cup in the Lord's hand (Jer. 51:7). She also is responsible for leading the nations away from God, by the wine of her fornication (Rev. 17:2).

> (18:4) And I heard another voice from heaven, saying, Come out of her, my people, that ye be not partakers of her sins, and receive not of her plagues. (5) For her sins have reached unto heaven, and God hath remembered her iniquities. (6) Reward her even as she rewarded you,... This is Babylon's judgment and God's recompense. (Rev. 18:4–6)

> For it is the vengeance of the Lord: take vengeance upon her, as she hath done, do unto her. (Jer. 50:15)

> Be not cut off in her iniquity; for this is the time of the Lord's vengeance, he will render her a recompense. (Jer. 51:6)

Therefore shall her plagues come in one day, death, and mourning, and famine; and she shall be utterly burned with fire: for strong is the Lord God who judgeth her … (11) And the merchants of the earth shall weep and mourn over her; for no man buyeth their merchandise any more. (Rev. 18:8, 11)

When Babylon is destroyed the world economic markets will collapse. She is utterly burned with fire, just the way Revelation 17:16 says the ten horns will do.

Alas, alas, that great city that was clothed in fine linen, and purple, and scarlet, and decked with gold, and precious stones, and pearls! (17) For in one hour so great riches is come to nought. And every shipmaster, and all the company in ships, and sailors, and as many as trade by sea, stood afar off. (18) And cried when they saw the smoke of her burning, saying, What city is like unto this city! (19) …wherein were made rich all that had ships in the sea by reason of her costliness [wealth], for in one hour is she made desolate. (Rev. 18:16–19)

Babylon the Great is a nation that is accessed by the sea, and because of her incredible wealth, anyone with a ship could trade with her and get wealthy. Old Babylon was never known for its sea merchants. Most of its trade and wealth came through land routes. It was located at a geographical hub. Note: she is wealthy at the time of her demise. Babylon will be great the day she is destroyed.

A common stumbling block for people studying Babylon is to think of her as just a "city." Babylon has never been just a city; it was a nation with one main capital city. Every great city has a nation to support it. No great city can exist without the resources of the surrounding land and citizens that live there. No single city could possibly buy all the world's merchandise and fulfill the scriptural requirements of Babylon the Great.

The question is, which nation reigns over the kings of the earth? This question will be explored in the next chapter on Babylon in this book.

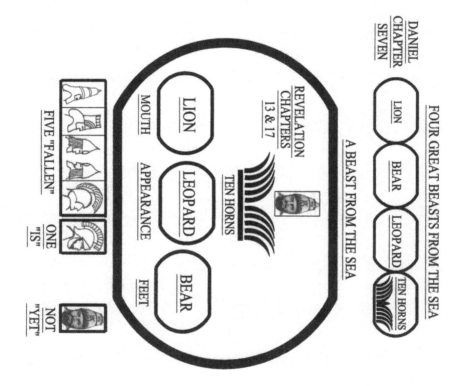

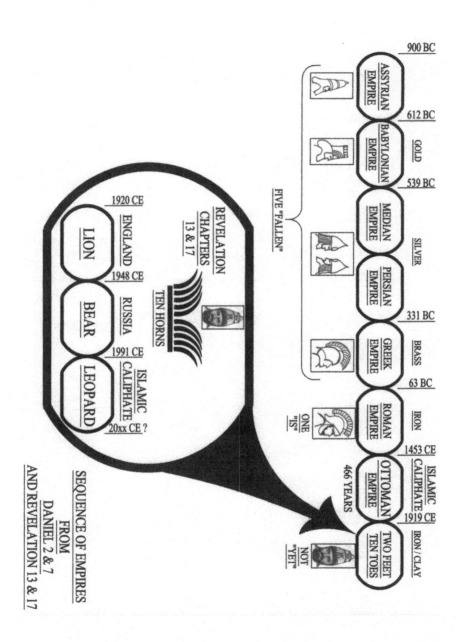

SEQUENCE OF EMPIRES
FROM
DANIEL 2 & 7
AND REVELATION 13 & 17

REVELATION
CHAPTERS
13 & 17

TEN HORNS

1920 CE
ENGLAND
LION
1948 CE
RUSSIA
BEAR
1991 CE
ISLAMIC
CALIPHATE
LEOPARD
20xx CE ?

FIVE "FALLEN"

900 BC
ASSYRIAN
EMPIRE

612 BC
BABYLONIAN
EMPIRE
GOLD

539 BC
MEDIAN
EMPIRE
SILVER
PERSIAN
EMPIRE

331 BC
GREEK
EMPIRE
BRASS

63 BC
ONE
"IS"
ROMAN
EMPIRE
IRON

1453 CE
OTTOMAN
EMPIRE
ISLAMIC
CALIPHATE

466 YEARS
NOT
"YET"
TWO FEET
TEN TOES
1919 CE
IRON / CLAY

87

CHAPTER SIX

Babylon the Great

It is necessary to have a scriptural understanding of Babylon in order to identify her properly. Prophecies concerning Babylon are not limited to the book of Revelation but are found in many locations in the writings of the Old Testament Jewish prophets. I will attempt to harmonize these prophecies in a concise and straightforward way.

Babylon began as the first kingdom after Noah's flood. Nimrod, the great hunter, founded the city of Babel as a place of refuge from wild animals and any threatening neighbors. God judged Babel because of their pride. God confounded the people's tongues because to make a name for themselves, they built a tower, the top of which would reach unto heaven. The Babylonians were scattered throughout the earth, becoming the nations, forming what has become known as the world. The term "world" is the Greek word *"kosmos"* and represents man's system of governments and institutions. They are opposed to God and must be removed before God's kingdom can be established on earth. The people of God live <u>within</u> this system but are not <u>of</u> this system (John 15:18–19). The people of God look for a city whose builder and maker is God (Heb. 11:10). The people of God clearly are told not to adopt the ways and actions of the kosmos:

> Love not the <u>kosmos</u>, neither the things that are in the <u>kosmos</u>.
> If any man love the , the love of the father is not in him. (16)
> For all that is in the <u>kosmos</u>, the lust of the flesh, and the lust
> of the eyes, and the pride of life, is not of the Father, but is of
> the <u>kosmos</u>. (17) and the <u>kosmos</u> passeth away, and the lust
> thereof: but he that doeth the will of God abideth for ever. (1
> John 2:15–17)

The kosmos is the system that God will dissolve when he sets up his kingdom, when the ten toes are destroyed by a stone cut out without hands.

> And there were great voices in heaven, saying, The kingdoms of
> this <u>kosmos</u> are become the kingdoms of our Lord and of his
> Christ, and he shall reign for ever and ever. (Revelation 11:15)

Babylon, as a nation, was a city-state located in Mesopotamia, the land between the Tigris and Euphrates Rivers, also known as the Valley of Shinar. This location today is the southern portion of Iraq. It was called a city-state because the city of Babylon was the capital, and the land around the city was the nation of Babylon, or Babylonia. The territory controlled by the city was constantly changing because of the strength of the surrounding nations. The kingdom and empire of Nebuchadnezzar is referred to by historians as the Neo Babylonian Empire, because it was revived from earlier Babylonian kingdoms. Neo Babylon existed from 604 BC until 539 BC, when the Medes and the Persians conquered Babylon. The term conquered is misleading, because there was little resistance—it actually was a non-battle. The Persians held Babylon until 331 BC, when Alexander the Great conquered it. He did not destroy it; instead, he set about to restore Babylon as his southern capital. Alexander's intended restoration, however, was never completed, because he fell ill and died in Babylon. The city of Babylon continued a gradual decline during the Hellenistic (Greek) period and was abandoned in ruins by 100 BC. The land around Babylon still is inhabited today, as a part of the modern nation of Iraq.

The Jewish prophets of Isaiah, Jeremiah, and Ezekiel all have prophecies about the fall or destruction of Babylon. I have reduced the prophecies to several points, with references to simplify what we should look for now, in our times. The references will include any direct cross-references from the New Testament. They are as follows:

1. Babylon existed at the time that Israel was re-established in 1948 (Isa. 14:1; Jer. 50:4–7, 51:19–20; Ezek. 17:22–24).
2. Babylon's national symbol is an eagle (Ezk. 17:7).
3. Babylon is the greatest economic nation in the world (Rev. 18:11, 17).
4. Babylon is the world's largest consumer nation (Rev. 18:11).
5. Babylon is the most powerful military nation (Jer. 50:23).
6. Babylon is a nation of mingled people—people from many nations woven together into one (Jer. 50:37).
7. Babylon was a golden cup in the Lord's hand, a nation used to bless the rest of the world (Jer. 51:7; Isa. 47:1).
8. Babylon becomes perverted. She trusts in her own wisdom and knowledge (Rev. 18:2; Isa. 47:1, 10; Jer. 51:7).
9. Babylon becomes a land given to idolatry (Jer. 50:38; 51:17, 18, 47, 52).
10. Babylon is a nation where the Jewish people will prosper and grow wealthy (Ezek. 17:8).
11. Babylon is the offspring of classical Babylon, the daughter of Babylon. She is not historical Babylon (Jer. 50:42; Jer. 51:33; Isa. 47:1; Rev. 18:20, 24).
12. Babylon is the hindermost of the nations, which means "end-time" or "last in time" (Jer. 50:12).
13. Babylon becomes full of the occult, witchcraft, and sorceries (Rev. 18:23; Isa. 47:9, 12, 13).
14. Babylon is proud. She considered herself a queen (Isa. 47:1; Rev. 18:7).
15. Babylon was called the "lady of kingdoms" (Isa. 47:5, 7).

The points made above will help to identify Babylon the Great. The points that follow highlight the judgment of Babylon.

1. Babylon is judged because of sin (Isa. 13:9, 11; Rev. 18:5, 8; Jer. 50:24).
2. God would have healed Babylon, but she is not healed (Jer. 50:8, 9).

3. Babylon is judged because of her treatment of the Jewish people (Jer. 50: 6,7; Isa. 47:6).
4. Babylon's judgment comes as a recompense and vengeance from God (Jer. 50:15, 28, 29; Jer. 51:6, 11, 24, 36, 56; Isa. 47:3).
5. The Lord God himself and his armies from heaven will come to execute judgment (Isa. 13:3, 5; Rev. 19:2, 11; Jer. 50:25).
6. At the fall of Babylon, the earth and the heavens shall be shaken; the sun, moon, stars, and the constellations shall not give their light. These signs are the same as found in Matthew 24:29, 30 and are related to the return of Jesus himself (Isa. 13:10, 13; Jer. 50:46).
7. The time of Babylon's judgment is known as the day of the Lord—the time of God's wrath and indignation. This time also is known as the tribulation period (Isa. 13:6, 9).
8. At the time of Babylon's judgment, the nation of Israel will be a great military power. God will use Israel as his battle axe and weapons of war against other nations (Jer. 51:20–22).
9. At the time of Babylon's judgment, all the world will be judged, and the nations of the world will gather together to do battle against God. This battle will be called Armageddon (Isa. 13:4, 11; Rev. 16:14).
10. Babylon will strengthen her national defenses, but it won't stop her destruction. Her defenses may even reach to the heavens (Jer. 51:12, 53).
11. At the time of Babylon's judgment, many people and merchants will flee back to their homelands (Isa. 13:14; Rev.18:15; Jer.50:8, 16; Jer. 51:6; Isa. 47:15).
12. Babylon will be attacked from her utmost, or northern, border (Jer. 50:3, 9, 26, 41; Jer. 51:27, 28, 48).
13. Babylon will be attacked by an assembly of great nations. They are stirred up against her. All the nations specifically named in Scripture fall within the modern borders of Iran and the old Soviet Union (Isa.13:17; Jer. 51:27, 28).
14. Babylon's military will be defeated and everyone found within her borders will be killed. There will be a great slaughter (Isa. 13:12, 15, 16; Rev. 18:22; Jer. 50:29–31, 35–37, 42; Jer. 51:3, 24, 30–32, 40, 57; Isa. 47:9).

15. Babylon will be completely desolate and will never be inhabited again (Isa. 13:20; Rev. 18:21, 22; Jer. 50:13, 39, 45; Jer. 51:29, 37, 43, 62; Isa 47:11).

It is impossible to reconcile the descriptions of Babylon's scriptural destruction to that of actual history. These prophecies were not fulfilled in historic Babylon; they were never meant to apply to historic Babylon. The fact that the book of Revelation was written some two hundred years after historic Babylon was abandoned and in ruins shows clearly that old Babylon is not the subject and that the prophecies place the events at the end of the age. The scope of this daughter of Babylon also is far beyond that of modern Rome, or Vatican City. It's hard to imagine Rome as a refuge for the Jews or the place where they would prosper and become a great nation. Also, Rome certainly is not the greatest economic/consumer nation of our times, nor is it the greatest military power.

Of all the nations existing in 1948 (the re-establishment of Israel), only one fits the descriptions of the daughter of Babylon, Babylon the Great. That is America. The following list shows how well America fits the description of Babylon the Great:

- America existed at the time of Israel's re-establishment in 1948.
- America's national symbol is an eagle. This symbol was established very early in America's history.
- America is the greatest economic nation in the world. America has by far the largest economy in the world. It is as large as all the European nations combined. America has a huge trade deficit and is buying more than it sells. If the American market suddenly were gone, the merchants of the earth would certainly cry, "No man buyeth our merchandise anymore."
- America is the most powerful military nation in the world—this is certainly true. She easily can be called the "hammer of the whole earth."
- America is a nation of mingled peoples, peoples woven together to be one. No nation in the world fits this description better than America. She is the melting pot of the world. Her national motto is E pluribus unum—"out of many, one."

- America has been a golden cup in the Lord's hand, a nation used to bless the rest of the world. America gives away approximately $25 billion in foreign aid each year. To put this into perspective, the Vatican has a total revenue of only a few hundred million dollars per year, approximately two-tenths of 1 percent of the amount America gives away. America also has been the source of most of the world's evangelistic missionary work. God certainly has used America to bless the world.

- America is a nation where the Jewish people have prospered and grown wealthy. Although the Jewish people have prospered in other nations, they always have had social and economic restrictions placed upon them. But in America, the melting pot of the world, they have the same opportunities as anyone else, and they have become a goodly vine. When the time came for God to re-establish the nation of Israel, it was the wealth of the American Jewish community that was instrumental in sustaining Israel. Yes, the Jewish people have been blessed in America.

Several descriptions of America are very negative and progressive, which I have chosen not to develop, such as, becoming perverted, being given to idolatry, and becoming full of the occult. I will leave it up to the reader to determine to what extent America fits these descriptions. . In my book *America, the Daughter of Babylon*, I develop these items and others in more detail.

There are actually three different battles related to the fall or destruction of Babylon, which takes place in the last days. The <u>first</u> is destruction and slaughter by the Assyrian and the ten commanders of his alliance. These hate the whore (Babylon) and burn her with fire and eat her flesh. This event also is seen in Jeremiah 50:9, where God says,

> For lo, I will raise up and cause to come against Babylon an <u>assembly of great nations</u> from the north country.

And again in Jeremiah 50:41, where we are told, "Behold a people shall come from the north, and a great nation, and <u>many kings</u> shall be raised up from the coasts of the earth."

The people of Babylon are slaughtered and many flee back to the nations from which they came.

> For fear of the oppressing sword they shall turn every one to his people, and they shall flee every one to his own land. (Jeremiah 50:16)

This battle caused great rejoicing in heaven, when they heard that the whore (Babylon the Great) was judged.

> And after these things I heard a great voice of much people in heaven, saying, Alleluia; Salvation, and glory, and honor, and power, unto the Lord our God: (2) For true and righteous are his judgments: for he hath judged the great whore, which did corrupt the earth with her fornication, and hath avenged the blood of his servants at her hand. (Revelation 19:1–2)

This scene in heaven precedes the return of the King of kings, with his bride and army, to the earth to fight the kings of the earth, and set up his kingdom. Later in Revelation 19:11, we see the heavens opened, and the Lord prepared to smite the nations and their armies.

In Isaiah 13, we find reference to the final destruction of Babylon, and we see that there are two aspects to it. One is the stirring up of the nation of the Medes, which is modern-day Iran, and it matches the destruction from the nations seen in Jeremiah. But the second aspect is the Lord himself and his army from heaven, which will destroy the whole land of Babylon.

> They come from a far country, from the end of heaven, even the Lord, and the weapons of his indignation, to destroy the whole land [Babylon]. (Isa. 13:5)

So God uses the nations of the earth to destroy Babylon, but the final and total destruction comes from God's army from heaven, and it happens later in time. It is the second battle and is called the day of the Lord.

A third battle against Babylon happens after the Messiah delivers his people from the place prepared for them in the wilderness, Edom.

He goes to Jerusalem and retakes the city from the Assyrian and his armies. The Messiah then assembles a command group of Israelis, and they attack and waste Assyria and Babylon. This the <u>third</u> destruction of Babylon. This account is found in Micah 5:5.

> And this man [the Messiah] shall be the peace, when the Assyrian shall come into our land [Israel]: and when he shall tread in our palaces, then shall we raise against him <u>seven shepherds and eight principal men</u>. (6) And they shall waste the <u>land of Assyria</u> with the sword, and the <u>land of Nimrod</u> [Babylon] in the entrances thereof: thus shall he [the Messiah] deliver us from the Assyrian, when he cometh into our land.

The destruction of the daughter of Babylon, the great whore (the first two battles), will be complete before Micah's account takes place. The land of Nimrod referred to in Micah 5 is the actual land of old Babylon (southern Iraq), which has not been destroyed by the assembly of great nations from the north. The daughter of Babylon is not old geographic Babylon found in Iraq, but rather another geographic location that is called the daughter of Babylon by God.

We have seen that America fits the description of the daughter of Babylon but does not openly bear that name. In Revelation 11, we find an account about two witnesses for God, who will be killed and left in the streets of the city. We are told that the city is spiritually called Sodom and Egypt. First of all, Sodom and Egypt are two different locations, so the names have nothing to do with geographic locations. The names are derived from the spiritual condition of the city, not its location. The account continues by telling us that the city is the same city in which our Lord was crucified—Jerusalem.

> And their dead bodies shall lie in the street of the great city, which spiritually is called Sodom and Egypt, where also our Lord was crucified. (Revelation 11:8)

<u>Babylon will be the spiritual name of America</u>, because of her perversions, idolatry, pride, and rebellion. This is the answer to the "mystery" of Babylon the Great. (Other spiritual and religious aspects to

Babylon fall outside the scope of this book but can be better understood from my book *America, the Daughter of Babylon*.)

Babylon the Great is seen in Revelation 17 as presiding over the beast and the ten horns of the final empire, until they, in their hatred, decide to destroy her. America can be seen in exactly that position with regard to NATO. NATO desires to be a European centered alliance and develop its European Security and Defense Identity (ESDI). NATO appreciates and has taken full advantage of using America's wealth and military assets, but it comes with a price. The Americans often see circumstances and policies differently than the Europeans see them and the Europeans have been forced to yield to—or at least to compromise with—the American position. they feel it should be Europeans making policies for Europe. Some American politicians have asserted that the Europeans are offended by what they perceive as American arrogance and meddling in European affairs.

What situation or event would cause NATO's future ten military commanders and their Assyrian leader to feel that they need to eliminate America, the woman? I believe the event is actually revealed in Daniel 11:30, when the ships of Chittim stop the Assyrian from moving unopposed into Israel. The Assyrian has to return home with his tail between his legs. We are told he is grieved and full of indignation. He has intelligence with the nations that forsake the holy covenant, and they support him against Chittim. When he returns to the south, there are no ships to stop him—they have been removed. He comes unopposed into Jerusalem. The only modern navy with that capability and a history of support and cooperation with Israel is America. This unilateral operation by America and its navy likely will be the trigger that causes the alliance to break down and the treachery to take place. Indeed, no nation, by itself, could destroy the hammer of the whole earth. If the European partners of NATO decided to turn on America, they would have the advantage of knowing all the defensive secrets needed to defeat her—she would be completely caught off guard.

> Behold, a people shall come from the north, and a great nation, and many kings shall be raised up from the coasts of the earth. (42) They shall hold the bow and the lance: they are cruel, and will not shew mercy: their voice shall roar like the sea, and

97

they shall ride upon horses, every one put in array, like a man to battle, against thee O <u>daughter of Babylon.</u> (43) The king of Babylon hath <u>heard the report</u> of them, and his hands <u>waxed feeble</u>: anguish took hold of him, and pangs as of a woman in travail. (Jeremiah 50:41–43)

When he hears the reports, the king of Babylon clearly is taken unaware and knows he has no options; the defeat is complete.

The great nation that anchors the military strike against Babylon can be identified in Scripture. This nation would need to have the military capability to strike North America from Europe and make a way for the army of Iran to invade and pillage the land. This is found in Jeremiah 51.

(27) Set ye up a standard in the land, blow the trumpet among the nations, prepare the nations against her [Babylon] the kingdoms of Ararat, Minni, and Ashchenaz ... (28) Prepare against her [Babylon] the nations with the kings of the Medes.

The nation of Ashchenaz is an ancient name for Russia. Even today, an Ashkenazi Jew is a Russian Jew. The nation of the Medes and Minni are in the modern-day nation of Iran. Minni is in the area of Iran that is near the old Assyrian kingdom, near lake Ermia. Ararat is in the northeastern portion of modern-day Turkey. These nations are a part of the great nations used to destroy the daughter of Babylon. It appears that Russia is the great nation that has the capability to destroy America from Europe. They probably don't even have to re-aim their ICBMs to hit American cities; they've been aimed at America for fifty years. Russia is now a NATO partner and is the bear of the final beast of Revelation 17. For modern-day Iran, America is the great Satan, and they would love nothing more than to destroy her.

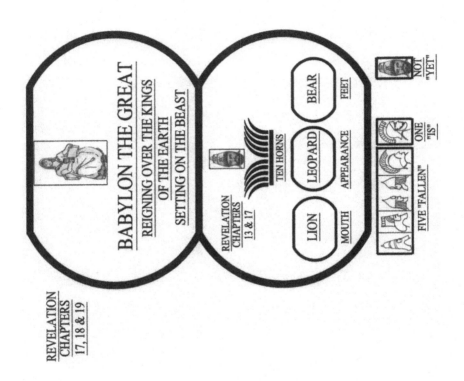

CHAPTER SEVEN

Things to Come

We have looked at the events of Daniel's visions that have been fulfilled and discussed how the remaining events may come to pass. I now want to look at some circumstances and situations that will need to change or at least develop before the end will come.

<u>The Jewish Temple</u>

The Jewish temple in Jerusalem, on the temple mount, where the abomination of desolation will be put by the Assyrian, does not exist today. This temple will exist prior to the last three and one-half years preceding Messiah's intervention to deliver his people. The Jewish temple was destroyed by the Romans in AD 70 and has not been rebuilt. The Moslems have built the Mosque of Omar on the mount, on or near the temple's old location. The mosque is an attempt to claim the temple mount as a Moslem holy site and prevent the Jews from building a new temple at that location. No temple would mean no abomination of desolation and no fulfillment of Daniel's vision.

The current Israeli government and a majority of the Jews living in modern-day Israel are not willing to provoke their Moslem neighbors by building on the mount. This situation will need to change before the temple can be built. I believe that the current militant Islamic movement, which is fueling the current instability in the Middle East, will need to be defeated before a Jewish temple can be built on the mount.

The book of Revelation that was received by John in approximately AD 90—shortly after the Romans destroyed the temple—has some interesting information about the temple that will exist during the time of the end. In Revelation 9 and 10, we find the accounts of the seven angels with seven trumpets. The seven trumpets announce the major events and judgments of God. In Rev. 11:1–2, John is told to take up a measuring reed and measure the temple.

> (1) And there was given unto me a reed like unto a rod: and the angel stood, saying, rise, and measure the temple of God, and the altar, and them that worship therein. (2) But the court which is without the temple leave out, and measure not; for it is given unto the gentiles: and the holy city shall they tread under foot forty and two months.

John is told to measure the temple building proper, which consists of the holy place and the holy of holies, or most holy place. He also is told to take note of them that worship within the temple. They would be the new Levitical priesthood, needed to perform the daily sacrifices, which is one of the primary functions of the temple. John also is told to measure the altar. There are two altars at the temple. One is the altar of incense, which is placed within the holy place, just in front of the holy of holies. The burning of incense before God represents the prayers of God's people, which is another primary function of the temple—a house of prayer. There is no need to measure the altar of incense because it clearly is defined by Scripture. But the second altar is the altar of sacrifice that is placed outside the temple building and is important to us because the Assyrian will cause the daily sacrifice to cease. The modern Jewish temple must be a full-service temple, which would include animal sacrifices. The idea of having a temple on the mount in Jerusalem may appeal to many Jews worldwide, but the reality of sacrificing animals on an altar would be a far more difficult thing for many Jews to accept.

The last thing John is told is not to measure the court that is without the temple. This court has been given to the Gentiles. Obviously, a compromise was made with regard to the use and control of the remaining area of the temple mount. It appears that the removal of the Mosque of Omar, the dome of the rock, may not need to happen. We are not told what the Gentiles will do with the rest of the mount, but it won't stop the Jews from sacrificing and worshipping in their temple. We further are told that the holy city will be trod under foot by the Gentiles for forty and two months, which is three and one-half years, or as Daniel states, time, times, and a half of time. This time frame clearly ties John's temple to the vision of Daniel.

I believe that this account in Revelation 11 is meant to clarify the components and the orientation of the end-time temple. It also clearly shows that the last Jewish temple is not a heavenly or spiritual temple, as believed by some scholars, but a real building located on the mount in Jerusalem. The actual dimensions of the temple are not important, because we are not given the dimensions taken by John; they are not included in Scripture. It should be noted, however, that the Jewish temple need not be very large or complicated to build. The temple building proper could be as small as 2,700 square feet in area, 90 feet long, 30 feet wide, and 45 feet high. The building has no systems, as we are used to seeing in modern churches and synagogues—no modern lighting system, no plumbing or air conditioning. It will not be wired for communications or sound systems. This will be a stone block building with wooden panels and gold veneer overlay. The building itself will be fabricated and assembled somewhere other than the temple mount and then disassembled and reassembled in place. The actual reassembly—the placement of the stone blocks—could happen overnight, with the fitting of the interior panels completed within days. The temple furniture probably is already complete and ready to be put in place.

I believe that the circumstances that will allow for the building of the last temple will come as a part of a comprehensive Middle East peace plan put forward by NATO (or whatever NATO will be called at that time), after the destruction of Damascus. The destruction of Damascus is seen in Isaiah 17:1:

> The burden of Damascus. Behold, Damascus is taken away from being a city, and shall be a ruinous heap.

This event has not happened; it is yet to take place. Damascus will be destroyed. This destruction may well be at the hands of the Israelis. They will be God's battle axe and weapons of war just prior to their own demise at the hands of the Assyrian.

> Thou [Israel] art my battle axe and weapons of war: for with thee will I break in pieces the nations, and with thee will I destroy kingdoms;...(4) And in that day it shall come to pass, that the glory of Jacob [Israel] shall be made thin, and the fatness of his flesh shall wax lean. (Jeremiah 51:20, 24)

The Israelis will understand the need to defend their land, but the thought that they are responsible for the destruction of a city will be devastating to their national psyche. They will be vulnerable to the peace proposals offered by NATO. Israel will yield their national defense by entering into an agreement (covenant) with NATO and NATO's Assyrian leader. One of the upside outcomes from this agreement will be the right for the Jews to have a place to worship on the temple mount.

NATO Transformation

Recently, NATO has become the tool of choice for America and Europe for the extension of military power around the world. NATO's original function was defensive. NATO was to prevent the Soviet Warsaw Pact nations from moving into Western Europe, a role that it has accomplished. Now, NATO has quietly transformed into an offensive military power that has conducted military operations not only in Europe but also in Asia and Africa. No other military alliance can compare to NATO in power and strength. The biggest problem NATO has at present is that Moslem nations perceive it as a revival of the European crusaders. In order to have any credibility in the Middle East, NATO needs to change its command and control system. Currently, NATO uses a consensus system to direct its forces, and each member nation has a representative to ensure that its views are heard. This system has functioned well, based on the old defensive mandate and easily defined objectives of the Cold War. While I don't believe that NATO needs to do away with the NATO Council for the maintenance and establishment of overall values and direction, it must streamline the military strike control. The ability to respond quickly to changing circumstances will require a smaller, more direct command group, able to direct assets on a moment's notice, all without consulting the NATO Council. To enhance credibility, this command group needs to better represent its member and partner nations. In short, it needs both Western and Eastern components—European and Middle Eastern commanders. Based on Scripture, I believe it will consist of five European generals and five Eastern generals (the ten toes of Daniel 2). Because this command group is inherently weak (part clay and part iron), an overall coordinator must bridge the gap—someone whom both sides would accept. Scripture indicates that he will be an Iranian Assyrian.

The 2011 NATO military action in Libya had the exact command problems as explained above, and one of the solutions suggested by NATO was an East/West command group. I believe this shows that the scenario is not far-fetched. For the interested observer, however, it is not always easy to know which decisions and directions are being considered within NATO. If you want to follow developments within NATO, there are third-party websites and also NATO's home site (nato. int), which can be helpful.

<u>American/European Relations</u>

The ten horns will hate the Babylonian whore and give their power and authority to the beast for the purpose of burning her with fire. Babylon is seen sitting atop the beast and ten horns. It is this presiding position that is the problem. America is the woman, and the ten horns represents the European and Eastern portion of the NATO alliance. Europe resents America's dominant global position and the fact that they often are not treated as equals. America uses its incredible wealth and military power like a big stick to push and get its way. Perceived American arrogance and meddling will continue to rub Europeans the wrong way. <u>This simmering conflict will begin to bubble to the surface more and more</u>. Eventually, this conflict will boil over when the American fleet (the ships of Chittim) act unilaterally against NATO and its leadership (the fourth Persian/Assyrian king) in support of Israel.

The Coming Persian/Assyrian Leader

Throughout this book, I've not used the term Antichrist to describe the final king of this world. The man who has been identified by so many people as the Antichrist is seen as the Antichrist for only the final three and one-half years of this age. This title is found only in the New Testament epistles of John, but he is identified more specifically in many other areas of Scripture. The name Antichrist is overused and distorted, but the Old Testament revelation and identification of him allows us to identify his nationality, his ethnic background, and his political affiliations and positions of power. These identifying factors will allow for his identification long before he becomes the Antichrist—the alternative to Christ.

He is a citizen of Iran and will be its leader, but he will have to change the rules, because he is not eligible to hold the office. He will come to power through a small people; I believe this refers to one of the minorities currently found in Iran. The minorities of Iran currently can hold a seat in Parliament but cannot be president or the supreme leader.

Ethnically, he will be an <u>Assyrian</u>. The Assyrian people are Semitic, the descendents of Shem. They lost their homeland (northern Iraq) to Islam during the Ottoman Empire, but have survived all attempts of genocide by the Moslems. There are currently about three million ethnic Assyrians scattered throughout the world, with about fifty thousand in Iran. If this man is alive today, it is highly likely that he is one of those fifty thousand. (Actually, the number is less than fifty thousand, because the Assyrian women would be eliminated from the count.) He is not just any Assyrian man; he is an Assyrian politician. He will be the leader of his people in Iran. This reduces the number of available candidates to just a handful of men.

He will be the man responsible for the establishment of a new Assyrian nation in the old Assyrian homeland. He will be more than just an Iranian Assyrian; he will be the <u>leader of an international movement to restore the Assyrians to their homeland</u>.

He will, at some point, have a relationship with NATO. He will be well suited to coordinate the ten commanders of NATO because he has Eastern connections through Iran and has Western connections through his Christian religion and Semitic background. He will be considered an articulate man with a policy of peace.

The underlined statements from the previous paragraphs contain many traits that can be used to identify the Assyrian prior to his becoming the Antichrist. I recommend following Assyrian news and developments online to keep informed.

The Islamic Caliphate

The level of stress and conflict between the Western world and the nation of Islam will become greater and more sharply defined until NATO needs to move into the Middle East to try to establish stability. Israel will have major deadly conflicts with her Moslem neighbors in the near future. The Arab spring will degrade into persecution for all but the most radical Moslems in the Middle East through the institution of sharia law.

The Lamb's Wife

The fourth chapter of this book makes reference to the Messianic deliverance of God's people from Edom. This is seen in Isaiah 63:1 and takes place in the "day of vengeance," the "year of my redeemed." This event also is described in Revelation 19:11 and is shown to take place after the marriage of the Lamb to his wife.

> Let us be glad and rejoice, and give honor to him: for the marriage of the Lamb is come, and his wife hath made herself ready. (8) And to her was granted that she should be arrayed in fine linen, clean and white: for the fine linen is the righteousness of saints. (Rev. 19:7–8)

The wife of the Lamb is the righteous saints of God, which are clothed in fine linen. The saints are not just espoused to the Lamb but are now his wife. They are now "one" with him and become part of his armies.

> And I saw heaven opened, and behold a white horse; and he that sat upon him was called Faithful and True, and in righteousness

he doth judge and make war. (12) His eyes were as a flame of fire, and on his head were many crowns; and he had a name written, that no man knew, but he himself. (13) And he was clothed with a vesture dipped in blood: and his name is called the word of God. (14) <u>And the armies which were in heaven followed him upon white horses, clothed in fine linen, white and clean.</u> (Rev. 19:11–14)

The battle that ensues is that great battle that ends the age. The beast, false prophet, and kings of the earth and their armies are defeated and judged.

And I saw the beast, and the kings of the earth, and their armies, gathered together to make war against him that sat on the horse, and against his army. (20) And the beast was taken, and with him the false prophet that wrought miracles before him, with which he deceived them that had received the mark of the beast, and them that worshipped his image. These both were cast alive into a lake of fire burning with brimstone. (21) And the remnant were slain with the sword of him that sat upon the horse, which sword proceeded out of his mouth: and all the fowls were filled with their flesh. (Rev. 19:19–21)

The armies of God—the wife of the Lamb—are in heaven prior to the destruction of Babylon the Great, because we see them rejoicing about the initial judgment and fall of the great whore, early in Revelation 19.

(1) And after these things [Babylon's judgment] I heard a great voice of much people <u>in heaven</u>, saying, Alleluia; Salvation, and glory, and honour, and power unto the Lord our God: (2) For true and righteous are his judgments: for he hath <u>judged the great whore</u> [also Rev.17]: which did corrupt the earth with her fornication, and hath avenged the blood of his servants at her hand. (3) and again they said, Alleluia. And <u>her smoke rose up for ever and ever</u> [also Rev 18].

After this celebration, the wife makes herself ready to return with the Lamb to earth, to fight the nations and assist Christ in setting up his kingdom. We know that the beast burns Babylon the Woman with fire, using the power and authority of the ten horns. The ten horns (or commanders) give their power to the beast for the whore's destruction because they hate her. This destruction will be a treacherous attack from NATO against America, to throw off American meddling in European affairs. The important fact to understand is the timing. The righteous saints (the wife) will have been in heaven for some time <u>before this attack</u>. How do they get there? When Jesus left this earth at the time of his Resurrection, he stated in John 14:2–3:

> (2) In <u>my father's house</u> [heaven] are many mansions: if it were not so, I would have told you. I go to prepare <u>a place for you</u>. (3) And if I go and prepare a place for you, <u>I will come again</u>, and receive you unto myself; that <u>where I am, there ye may be also</u>.

This promise to his followers is called the blessed hope (expectation). For thousands of years Christians have looked forward to the day that he would return to take the righteous home. This event is further described by the apostle Paul in 1 Thessalonians 4.

> (16) For the Lord himself shall descend <u>from heaven</u> with a shout, with the voice of the archangel, and the trump of God: and the <u>dead in Christ shall rise first</u> [resurrect]: (17) Then <u>we which are alive and remain shall be caught up together</u> with them in the clouds, to meet the Lord in the air: and so <u>shall we ever be with the Lord</u>.

This resurrection is for the purpose of gathering the righteous believers to heaven for the marriage of the Lamb. These believers are not just Jews but come from every nation and every tongue.

> After this [the sealing of 144,000 Jews] I beheld , and lo, a great multitude, which <u>no man could number,</u> of <u>all nations,</u> and kindreds, and people, and tongues, stood <u>before the throne,</u> and

before the Lamb, clothed with white robes, and palms in their hands; (10) And cried with a loud voice, saying, Salvation to our Lord which sitteth upon the throne, and unto the Lamb.... (14)...These are they which came out of great tribulation, and have washed their robes, and made them white in the blood of the Lamb. (Rev. 7:9–10, 14)

The key to their righteousness is the blood of the Lamb. They are washed by the blood (sacrifice) of the lamb. This truth is seen in Isaiah 53.

(7) He [the Messiah] was oppressed, and he was afflicted, yet he opened not his mouth: he is brought as a lamb to the slaughter,... (8)...for he was cut off out of the land of the living: for the transgression of my people was he stricken....(10)Yet it pleased the LORD to bruise him; he hath put him to grief: when thou shalt make his soul and offering for sin....(11) He shall see of the travail of his soul, and shall be satisfied: by his knowledge shall my righteous servant justify many; for he shall bear their iniquity. (12)...he hath poured out his soul unto death;....and made intercession for the transgressors.

The sacrifice of this righteous servant made the way for people of all nations to become the wife of the Lamb and escape the wrath of God in the final days of this age. God is calling to men of every nation and family to wash their sins away by acknowledging and applying the blood of this perfect sacrifice. Pray to this Jewish Messiah that you may be found worthy of escaping the wrath of God.

Watch ye therefore, and pray always, that ye may be accounted worthy to escape all these things that shall come to pass, and to stand before the Son of man. (Luke 21:36)

The precise time of this event cannot be predicted, but the times can be seen. In Luke 21, Jesus is explaining the events at the end of the age to his disciples. He lists the signs that will happen to usher in the kingdom of God. He also states that at the beginning of these events, the believers are to look up, because their redemption is very close.

And when these things <u>begin</u> to come to pass, <u>then look up</u>, and lift up your heads; for your redemption draweth nigh. (Luke 21:28)

The removal of the righteous saints which are espoused to the lamb will take place just prior to God's judgment on Babylon the Great. We don't know the precise time, but there are indications that it will surprise those who are not vigilant. Life can move along pretty much as normal, at least on the surface, but God could decide to call his bride home, because his wrath will be coming in the morning.

Therefore <u>be ye also ready</u>: for in such an hour as <u>ye think not</u> the Son of man cometh. (Matthew 24:44)

Likewise also as it was in the days of Lot; they did eat, they drank, they bought, they sold, they planted, they builded. (29) But <u>the same day</u> that Lot went out of Sodom it rained fire and brimstone from heaven, destroyed them all. (30) Even <u>thus shall it be</u> in the day when the Son of man is revealed. (Luke 17:28–30)

Life in Sodom was completely normal, and everyone was doing what they do every day. They were not expecting God's judgment on that morning, and they did not miss Lot and his family, whom God's angel had removed. The catching away of God's elect bride might go mostly unnoticed by the world at large, because people are too busy dealing with the sudden cataclysmic changes and world events.

In closing this book, I exhort my readers to consider carefully which side of the final battle they wish to be on—the kings of this world and their armies, or the Lord of Hosts and his armies. Your future will be radically different, depending on your choice. Ask God to forgive your sin and prepare you to live as his righteous servant until you receive his call to come home. Apply the perfect blood sacrifice of God's righteous servant to your life, and put your trust in Christ Jesus, the only begotten of the Father.

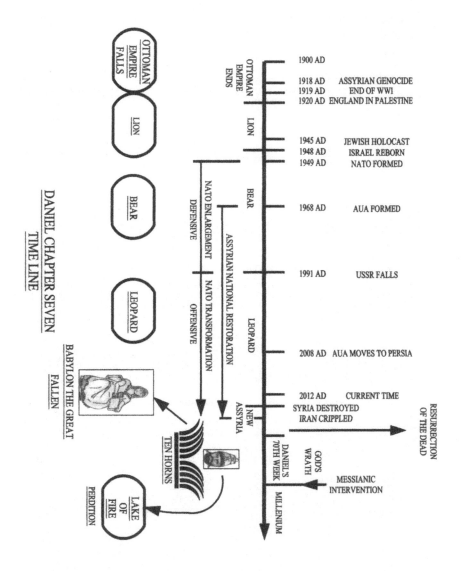

DANIEL CHAPTER SEVEN
TIME LINE

GENERAL INDEX

Kosmos: 89, 90

Lambs wife: 107, 108
Leopard: 33, 34, 40, 42, 44, 69, 70, 86, 87, 99, 112
Lion: 33, 34, 40, 44, 48, 49, 69, 79, 86, 87, 99, 112
Little horn: 1, 23, 24, 29, 35, 36, 38, 39, 44, 48, 60, 62, 65, 71

MENE TEKEL UPHARSIN: 8

NATO: 1, 45-50, 81, 97, 98, 103-107, 112
NATO Russia council (NRC): 46
Nebuchadnezzar's image: 4-6, 9, 11, 12, 69

Resurrection: 109

Sharia law: 9, 10, 42
Son of Man: 36, 37
Symbol of Asshur: 76

Temple mount: 24
Ten horns: 34, 35, 40, 44, 48, 60, 62, 66, 68, 69, 81, 86, 87, 99, 105, 112
The false prophet: 71
The indignation: 26
The vile king: 52, 53, 57, 59, 63, 71

Warsaw pact: 45
World War I: 10, 40
World War II: 45, 54

INDEX OF NAMES

INDEX OF PLACES

SCRIPTURE INDEX